the Kings' Tales

the Kings' Tales

Phillip and Robert King

B. T. Batsford Ltd, *London*

First published 1994

© Phillip and Robert King 1994

ISBN 0 7134 7645 1

A CIP catalogue record for this book is available from the British Library.

Typeset by Apsbridge Services Ltd, Nottingham.
Printed by Redwood Books, Trowbridge, Wiltshire
for the publishers,
B. T. Batsford Ltd, 4 Fitzhardinge Street,
London W1H 0AH

A BATSFORD BRIDGE BOOK
Series Editor: Tony Sowter

CONTENTS

INTRODUCTION

An expert whose ego was legendary was playing in a big tournament with a promising pupil. He stared arrogantly round the room and remarked, "Only one player here is in my class – Forquet." Two rounds later they found themselves playing against the famous Italian, who promptly floored an easy game. The pupil nodded sagely at his expert and said, "I see what you mean."

Now that story could have been told about most sports, but it happens to be just right for bridge, which, perhaps because it is so demanding and exasperating, exposes most aspects of human folly. It is no wonder that the game inspires more humorous writing than any other.

In recognition of that tradition, this book contains parodies and pastiches of famous player-writers and other authors whose styles are ideal for portraying different facets of the game.

For the literary minded, a parody, according to Dr. Johnson, takes the work of an author and, while remaining faithful to the style, adapts it for some new purpose. According to Tim Stanley-Clamp, who helped edit this book, a pastiche is somewhat gentler; it imitates, rather than changes the original, and is therefore a form of tribute.

Somerset Maugham said that he hated people who played bridge as though they were at a funeral and knew their feet were getting wet. What follows was written for those who agree with Mr. Maugham.

1
PHILIP MARLOWE

Raymond Chandler was a Dulwich schoolboy who went to America and became the back-street poet who raised the tough detective story to the level of literature. He was master of the one liner.

"She was a blonde. A blonde to make a Bishop kick a hole in a stained glass window."

"I left her with her virtue intact, but it was quite a struggle. She nearly won."

"A bitter, hard boiled city with no more personality than a paper cup."

"All the simple old-fashioned charm of a cop beating up a drunk."

He could be hard on his fellow writers: "Conan Doyle and Edgar Allen Poe were primitives in their art. The Purloined Letter would not fool a modern cop for four minutes." And he wrote of James Bond, "I like him least when he takes the beautiful girl in his arms and teaches her about one tenth of the facts of life she knew already."

Chandler's detective was Philip Marlowe, who loved chess, but preferred to study it alone by replaying the games of Capablanca and Alekhine. He was too solitary to have played much bridge, yet he could have been outstanding. He was tough, cool, impassive, courageous, analytical and unorthodox.

And above all, as he admitted in The Big Sleep, he was not always a gentleman.

Double is My Business

The Bay City Country Club reeked of new money. It had all the taste and refinement of a Texas Whorehouse. I sat at the bar and blew smoke at the ornate murals. It didn't make them disappear but it helped. I sipped slowly at a small bourbon. Two minutes ago it had been a large bourbon.

Someone sat down at the next stool. He was a grey man, all grey, except for his sad blue eyes. His face was so long he could have wrapped it round his waist. He spoke in a soft grey voice. "Philip Marlowe?"

I gave him my best grey smile and my card, the one without the machine gun in the top right corner.

"I'm Dwight Romaine," he said. "I hope I haven't kept you waiting."

I told him not to worry. I had all the time in the world. I was as busy as an entertainments officer in a Trappist monastery.

"You come highly recommended, Mr. Marlowe," he said. "I'm told that you are very discreet."

I said nothing, but I reassured him by taking a discreet pull at my bourbon. He got the message and ordered two more.

"What did Bernie Ohls tell you?" he asked.

I waited discreetly until the bartender had ambled out of earshot. "Bernie told me you were being blackmailed," I said. "Quite probably by someone who plays bridge at this club. The last time you played you left a compromising letter at the table. One of the other players must have taken it. It happens all the time."

"Very succinct." He looked at his watch. "The afternoon game starts in three minutes. The same happy foursome, would you believe? Do you play bridge Mr. Marlowe?"

I didn't deny it.

"How would you like to take my place for a rubber or two? It will give you the opportunity to meet the suspects."

"What are the stakes?"

"Very modest. A dollar a point. The average rubber is around a thousand. We settle by cheque at the end of the session."

I tried to look as if this was chicken feed. I was Gaylord Marlowe, the riverboat gambler. I thought nothing of staking the family plantation on one roll of dice. If I lost I could always blow my brains out. I wouldn't miss them.

"Tell me where you all sat for the last rubber."

He told me, and we went into the card room. It was decorated in a lavish blend of Art Decco and Cubist Revival. By comparison the bar seemed moderately understated.

There were three people at the bridge table. He introduced them. "This is a friend of mine, Philip Marlowe. Miss Delmar, Mr. Schultz, Mr. Carillo."

Schultz was no more than six feet eight tall and as wide as a con-man's smile. Hard, black eyes gazed at me from a hard, mean face. He looked as if he could talk and spit without bothering the cigar that lived in his mouth.

Carillo was shuffling the cards. His long fingers were so fast they made a casino dealer look like an arthritic turtle. He was a dark handsome Latin with a neat black moustache and enough jewellery to stock a counter at Tiffany's. His eau de cologne would have neutralised a herd of mountain goats. A real homewrecker.

Miss Delmar was trouble. She had hot, black eyes and an ice cold stare. Her hair was red and matched her full sensuous lips. Her smile would have made Leonardo tear up the Mona Lisa and start again. Her legs were a tone poem in sheer silk and she had them arranged to be stared at. I stared.

"I'm afraid I have to meet a business associate," said Romaine. "Mr. Marlowe has kindly agreed to play until I return. If nobody objects."

Nobody objected. We cut for partners. By coincidence, the others had the same seats as for the last rubber with Romaine.

I faced Miss Delmar. "What do you play, Mr. Marlowe?" She made it sound like an erotic invitation.

I replied in my best life master manner. "Culbertson, strictly by the Blue Book. Not Blackwood. He's for palookas."

"Poor Easley," she drawled. "A pity, Mr. Marlowe. He speaks very highly of you."

I let that one pass and watched Carillo's rapid mechanic's shuffle. Schultz cut the cards. In his hands they looked like five cent stamps. I dealt and found myself looking at a rock crusher:

♠AK ♡AQ107432 ◇A104 ♣A

I opened two hearts, game forcing. Miss Delmar raised to four. I wondered what that meant. I gave up wondering and bid the small slam. Carillo doubled. He led ◇J and dummy went down. It wasn't the worst double raise I've ever seen, but it came close.

♠ 9843
♡ J85
◇ K76
♣ Q94

♠ AK
♡ AQ107432
◇ A104
♣ A

Contract 6♡. ◇J led.

"An interesting raise," I remarked.

"I thought it was routine," she smiled. "It shows trump support but not much else. Three hearts would show more strength. I learned that from Easley."

I thanked her with all the sincerity of a Huey Long election pledge. But I had to admit that after the ◇J lead the slam looked frigid. All I had to do was rise with the ◇K and finesse the ♡Q. If it lost, dummy's ♡J would be an entry to take the marked diamond finesse. If it won, I could drive out Schultz's ♡K and still have my entry. Child's play.

But hold on Marlowe, I thought. You're supposed to be a detective. Why did Carillo double? And why did he lead the ◇J? Was it a singleton? He couldn't expect Schultz to have the ace. If I had any controls missing I would have started cue bidding and to hell with Easley.

I looked at his face. It was dark, deep and devious. I laid odds on his double being based on the guarded ♡K and all the missing honours. The ◇J was a false card, and a good one. It nearly fooled the great Shamus.

The hand turned out to be the perfect set up for a squeeze:

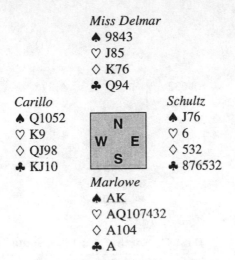

Miss Delmar
♠ 9843
♡ J85
◇ K76
♣ Q94

Carillo
♠ Q1052
♡ K9
◇ QJ98
♣ KJ10

Schultz
♠ J76
♡ 6
◇ 532
♣ 876532

Marlowe
♠ AK
♡ AQ107432
◇ A104
♣ A

I took in hand with the ◇A. I played the ♡A and ♡Q. Carillo won and led a spade. I reeled off winners. The end position was a text book classic.

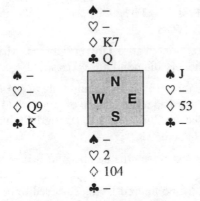

♠ –
♡ –
◇ K7
♣ Q

♠ –
♡ –
◇ Q9
♣ K

♠ J
♡ –
◇ 53
♣ –

♠ –
♡ 2
◇ 104
♣ –

When I led the ♡2, Carillo was squeezed as flat as Fred Astaire's top C.

As I took my twelfth trick I snuck a glance at Miss Delmar, trying not to look like a poodle hoping to be patted.

"Well played Mr. Marlowe." She rewarded me by uncrossing her legs and crossing them again. I couldn't see the result but my imagination was on overdrive.

Carillo was frowning as he dealt the next hand:

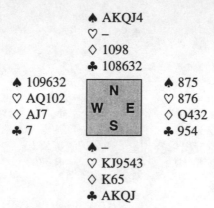

```
              ♠ AKQJ4
              ♡ –
              ◇ 1098
              ♣ 108632
♠ 109632                      ♠ 875
♡ AQ102       N              ♡ 876
◇ AJ7       W   E            ◇ Q432
♣ 7           S              ♣ 954
              ♠ –
              ♡ KJ9543
              ◇ K65
              ♣ AKQJ
```

North/South Game. Dealer East.

West	North	East	South
Schultz	*Marlowe*	*Carillo*	*Delmar*
–	–	Pass	1♡
Pass	1♠	Pass	2◇
Pass	3◇	Pass	3NT
All Pass			

The bidding had more holes than a Gruyere cheese. Miss Delmar's 2◇ was a cute semi-psyche. My diamond raise was strictly for canaries.

Schultz chewed his bottom lip as he thought about his lead. Finally he produced the ♣7. Delmar had more chance of getting into Fort Knox than into dummy. She called for dummy's ♣8, covered Carillo's ♣9 with the ♣K and immediately led the ◇K.

Schultz frowned. This just wasn't his day. Like a British heavyweight, he forgot to duck and won with the ◇A. He placed Carillo with ♣QJ9x and declarer with ♣AKx. So he figured Delmar needed three tricks from the red suits and he wasn't about to make things easy for her. He led a small spade.

Delmar was on table. She gave me a knowing smile and cashed her winning spades discarding ♣AQJ. Now dummy's clubs were good and nine tricks rolled in.

I uncrossed my legs and crossed them again, but she didn't seem to notice. "Thank you partner," I said. "You played that like a goddess."

"Thank you, Mr. Marlowe. The defence was kind to me. I make that a rubber of 1,710."

Romaine was back. "Congratulations," he said. "May I have a word with you before I take your place?"

It was time to drop a small bombshell. "About the blackmailer?" I asked.

They all looked at me. Romaine seemed pained, Schultz puzzled, Carillo poker faced, Delmar faintly amused.

"It's a simple case," I explained. "Last week someone at this table stole a letter from Mr. Romaine." I blew out some cigarette smoke to let the accusation sink in. There was no reaction. They were all as hard as a loan shark's heart.

I turned to Romaine. "I take it you lost last week?"

His sad eyes grew sadder. "The cards were not kind to me."

"So you wrote out a cheque?"

"Naturally."

"You're left-handed of course."

"How do you know that, Mr. Marlowe?"

"You have some fancy bridgework on the right side of your mouth and none on your left. You can always spot a left-handed brusher."

"That's very clever."

"So your notecase was at your left when you wrote the cheque. You kept the letter in it?"

"Yes."

"So there it was, next to the golden arm of Carillo. He could snatch it so fast you wouldn't see his hand move."

There was a pause. Carillo froze. Delmar broke the silence. "You intrigue me, Mr. Marlowe. You see, Mr. Romaine is not the only one who is being blackmailed."

"He sure as hell ain't," said Schultz. He glanced at Carillo and eased back his chair. He growled. It must have registered high on the Richter scale.

Carillo leapt to his feet. His hand snaked towards his shoulder holster. He was fast, but not fast enough. My police .38 was already pointing at him from beneath the table.

A gentleman would have given him a fighting chance. I didn't. I fired twice. He reached both hands to his chest. They were fine hands, talented hands, but they were no use to him. He fell forward, dead.

I left ten minutes later. I didn't know what they would tell the police but the Bay City Country Club probably owned the police. I expected to learn next day that Carillo died of food poisoning.

I drove home in the fine autumn rain. I felt a little cleaner. I had a big cheque from Romaine and seventeen hundred and ten dollars they had taken from Carillo's bankroll. That seemed fair. It was a bad double.

And there was a note from Miss Delmar. I read it while I stopped at a traffic light.

> Dear Mr. Marlowe,
>
> I think the best way to thank you is to recommend a book. It's called Bridge Harmonics. It's by Easley. Perhaps you'd care to ring me when you've read it.
>
> Yours,
>
> Ruth Delmar.

I smiled and turned the car round. If I drove quickly I might find a bookstore open.

2
RUNYON ON ZIA

Zia Mahmood is a guy who likes to write about Damon Runyon charac-ters more than somewhat. And I will lay you plenty of six to four that he is a Runyon Character himself, or maybe more so.

A few years ago he is voted the World's Bridge Personality of the Decade, and I do not have to tell you that the world is a very big place and a decade is a very long time indeed, especially if you are in the sneezer. He is also a scribe who writes a book called Bridge My Way, *though only a real sucker will figure him to write a book called* Bridge Someone Else's Way.

He plays the odd rubber in uptown New York, where he is known to win a few potatoes to take care of the old overhead. I hear from guys who know about such things that Zia is not a dude who leads low from AK3 against six no trumps, but you are always thinking he might at that, as he is par-tial to the old phonus bolonus. This makes him a very hard guy to figure and is why certain citizens are wearing last year's neckties and have no scratch to bet on the horses or spend on the dolls.

Zia on Broadway

I was playing rubber bridge in New York. My partner was a Damon Runyon character called Louis the Lip. Louis had his good points and his bad points. He was arrogant and opinionated and thought he was God's gift to bridge. Because of all this I always overlooked his bad points.

As we cut for the deal, Louis told me how last time he played he had been dealt thirteen spades. One of our opponents was Bernie Finklestein, a shrewd gambler and a real sceptic, the kind of guy who never accepts a claim unless he can see that declarer has five overtricks. His motto was:

the race may not always be to the swift, but that's the way to bet.

"Louis," he said. "Listen. You have less chance of holding all thirteen spades than I have of becoming the next Jewish Pope, and that is a very small chance indeed. I am not saying you tell a lie, but it will do very well until a lie comes along. So, I make you a proposition. If ever you are again dealt all thirteen spades I will let you sleep with my ever-loving wife."

Louis laughed, "Bernie, I will hold you to that."

The cards were dealt and Louis the Lip, in fourth position after three passes, found himself looking at ♠AKQJ1098765432. At that precise moment, a woman walked into the club and waved at Bernie. He waved back and said, "Gentlemen, I would like that you say a big hello to my wife, Thelma."

Louis' response was instantaneous. "No bid!" he said.

When I told this story on TV I was accused of being sexist. This is a crazy notion, and to prove it I am going to tell you about a time when a lovely lady, called Simone, out-thought me three times out of four.

Love All. Dealer West

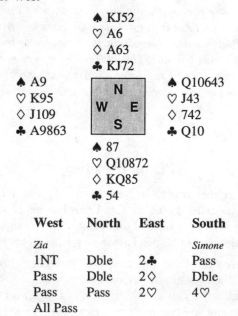

```
              ♠ KJ52
              ♡ A6
              ◇ A63
              ♣ KJ72
  ♠ A9          N        ♠ Q10643
  ♡ K95       W   E      ♡ J43
  ◇ J109        S        ◇ 742
  ♣ A9863                ♣ Q10
              ♠ 87
              ♡ Q10872
              ◇ KQ85
              ♣ 54
```

West	North	East	South
Zia			*Simone*
1NT	Dble	2♣	Pass
Pass	Dble	2◇	Dble
Pass	Pass	2♡	4♡
All Pass			

East was trying to wriggle to 2♠, but Simone was not impressed and bid the heart game.

I am often asked if writing and broadcasting about my favourite deceptive plays makes them less effective at the table. Well, it can work both ways, as we shall see.

I led the ♠9. Simone knew all about my phony nines. She gave me a faint smile and rose with the ♠K. She played the ♡A and I followed with the ♡9. If this was a true card, of course declarer's only chance would be to continue with a heart to the queen since she cannot pick up ♡J543, but she smiled again, led another heart and finessed the ♡10. In with the ♡K, I switched to the ♣9. Simone's smile was by now a beam of pleasure. She played the ♣K from dummy and continued with a small diamond to her ◇K.

At this point I played not the nine, but the ◇10. She drew trumps, and crossed to dummy's ◇A, on which I dropped the jack, still preserving my precious nine. Now Simone led dummy's last diamond and confidently finessed the ◇8. I took the trick, cashed my two aces and wrote one hundred above the line, taking care not to smile.

North was not pleased. "Why did you play the diamonds against the odds?"

"Because I thought Zia didn't have the nine, or he'd have played it."

"But you had a virtual count of the hand. Zia had three hearts, presumably two spades, and at most five clubs, so if he didn't have a third diamond he must have been a card short. Did you think he'd been dealt twelve?"

Simone's smile returned. "With Zia you never know," she said.

3
FIRST GENTLEMAN

Terence Reese is regarded by many as the greatest player Britain has ever produced and in his prime was arguably one of the best in the world. He is also a prolific and versatile writer, many of whose works have become classics.

One of the best examples of his laconic wit is recounted in Bridge at the Top. *He was playing at his club during the Blitz of 1940. After a violent explosion had rocked the building, an agitated member in uniform rushed into the room and cried, "They've hit the War Office!" "Not intentionally," said Reese.*

His parents met at a whist drive, where they were introduced as the 'first lady' and 'first gentleman'.

Reese on Form

A correspondent from somewhere North of Watford writes, "The enclosed deal may interest your reader". His memory is evidently as deficient as his singular wit, as no hand was attached, so I decided to substitute the following curiosity from a 1932 Gold Cup match, in which I occupied the West seat:

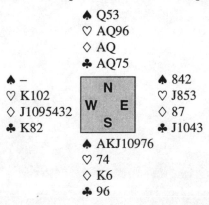

```
                  ♠ Q53
                  ♡ AQ96
                  ◇ AQ
                  ♣ AQ75
    ♠ –                        ♠ 842
    ♡ K102          N          ♡ J853
    ◇ J1095432   W     E       ◇ 87
    ♣ K82            S         ♣ J1043
                  ♠ AKJ10976
                  ♡ 74
                  ◇ K6
                  ♣ 96
```

The bidding was typical of the period:

West	North	East	South
3◊	3NT	Pass	6♠
All Pass			

I pondered my choice of lead. South was the late Hugo Carruthers, an undistinguished barrister who, had he been able to devote more time to bridge, would have been even less successful at the bar. I pondered my choice of lead and recalled a maxim from one of my early books – I think it was *Reese on Leads* – 'When in doubt lead a trump'. Old hat, you say? Perhaps, but in 1929 it was pretty hot stuff.

I was about to follow my own advice when it suddenly dawned on me that I had no trump. Fortunately, I remembered a ploy from another of my books, *Reese on Deception*, and selected the ♡10.

Hugo studied this card with forensic suspicion. Was it a singleton? Or was I capable of something more subtle? Remember that this was before I had scored the first of my eight Gold Cup wins. Eventually, he rose with the ♡A. You don't approve? Perhaps not, but this was several years before the publication of *Reese on Approval*.

Boris, my partner, frowned. I should explain that this was before the first of his nine Gold Cup victories, an achievement with which he was always taunting me, even then. He played the ♡8, reinforcing my deception, and I thanked my stars that I had made him read *Reese on Signalling*.

Hugo confidently drew trumps and played two rounds of diamonds, finishing in hand. He then led the ♡7, reading my ♡2 as the second card of a doubleton, and triumphantly finessed the ♡9, smiling complacently at what he thought was a masterly end-play. In with the ♡J, Boris returned a nonchalant ♡5. Hugo discarded a club and I made the setting trick with my ♡K.

A rather interesting feature of this otherwise jejune example of medieval defence was that when my ♡K landed innocently on the table, Hugo had a cardiac arrest, and we had to play the last eight boards against a substitute.

Poor Hugo bore a superficial resemblence to the abrasive Humphrey Hoosego, a character in *Bridge with Mr. Playbetter*, which I wrote with Hubert Phillips. The next hand shows the insufferable Humphrey in action. It is rather juvenile, but it gave our readers, some of whom were under forty, the pleasure of watching him writhe in agony.

A Bad Day for Hoosego

Hoosego was having a wretched afternoon. The cards were not running for him, and he was playing below his usual form. Then he cut the redoubtable General Trumpington against Mrs Hart-Stopper and Lady Passmore, who were frequent victims of his sarcastic wit.

The men had a part-score of 60 when Humphrey dealt the following hand:

General Trumpington
♠ K65
♡ 1074
♢ A8
♣ KJ852

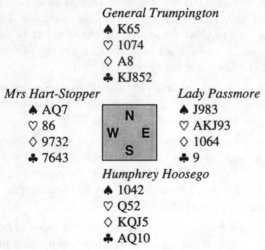

Mrs Hart-Stopper
♠ AQ7
♡ 86
♢ 9732
♣ 7643

Lady Passmore
♠ J983
♡ AKJ93
♢ 1064
♣ 9

Humphrey Hoosego
♠ 1042
♡ Q52
♢ KQJ5
♣ AQ10

Hoosego, adding a point for his tens, and a couple more for his dummy play, opened a strong no trump, which was passed out.

On lead, Mrs Hart-Stopper thought furiously. Last week, Humphrey had remarked that everything she knew about defence could be written in the margin of a postage stamp and still leave room for Ranjitsinjhi's autograph, and she was determined to avenge the insult. After a meaningful look at the part-score, the General had passed smugly, so a bold defence was indicated. Finally, she chose the ♠Q as the card most likely to mislead declarer.

Hoosego, supposing the lead to be from QJ9, played low from both hands. When the ♠7 was continued, he played low from dummy again and gnashed his teeth when East's ♠J won the trick.

Lady Passmore could now place her partner with the ♠A, and declarer with every missing honour, and it seemed that the defence could come to no more than six tricks – four spades and two hearts. She reflected that only yesterday Hugo had remarked that she was to bridge what Dame

Margot Fonteyn was to oxy-acetylene welding. Smarting at the recollection, she led a wicked ♡J!

Humphrey was mystified. He envisaged every possible distribution but the actual one. The most likely, he thought, was that West held a doubleton honour, so he ducked, hoping the suit would be blocked.

Triumphantly, Lady Passmore followed with a spade to her partner's ace, won the heart return and sadistically reeled off her major suit winners, to defeat the contract by three tricks.

The general stared at his partner with an expression of bellicose disbelief. In an attempt to divert his military wrath towards their opponents, Hoosego turned to Mrs Hart-Stopper. "What a monstrous opening lead!" he snarled.

"I think I read it somewhere," she replied demurely. "Probably on the margin of a postage stamp."

4
THE DEVIL'S DICTIONARY

In 1913, a seventy-one-year old American adventurer went to Mexico to join the revolutionary forces of Pancho Villa. He was never seen or heard of again.

He was the writer Ambrose Bierce, whose works include collections of aphorisms called The Devil's Dictionary *and* The Cynic's Word Book. *His definitions of 'acquaintance' and 'noise' are fine examples of his style.*

Acquaintance (n)
A person whom we know well enough to borrow from but not well enough to lend to.

Noise (n)
A stench in the ear. The chief product and authenticating sign of civilisation. (As all duplicate players know, this led directly to the invention of bidding boxes.)
Bierce would have found bridge a fertile field for his talent:

The Devil's Bridge Dictionary

Contract Bridge
A game which allows couples to inflict mental torture on each other in public, without incurring criminal charges or social ostracism.

Partner
A person who collaborates with your opponents to ensure that you lose heavily.

Above the Line
A portion of the scorecard intended primarily for recording the consequences of the greed, poor judgement and gross stupidity of one's partner.

S O S Redouble
An appeal to partner to rescue you from a hopeless situation, often mistaken as expression of satisfaction with that situation.

Master Points
A reward for the triumph of persistence over ability.

Grand Master
An expert who has added longevity to those two qualities.

Expert
A person who invariably knows the correct play as soon as he has made the wrong one.

Palooka
A derogatory name given by a bridge player to those who are worse than he is and to some who are better.

Club Professional
A player who is paid a stipend as partial compensation for his rubber bridge losses.

Part-score
A device designed to confuse duplicate players who foolishly enter the domain of rubber bridge experts.

Post Mortem
An attempt to demonstrate that the unsuccessful play one has chosen is theoretically superior to the successful alternative one failed to notice.

Flitch
A form of mixed pairs, lacking the high level of tolerance seen in other forms.

Forcing Pass
An act of abdication compelling partner to choose between equally unattractive alternatives.

Grand Slam
An ambitious contract which should be called only if thirteen tricks are probable, or if partner is to play the hand, inevitable.

Master Bid
A bid which is so ingenious that it enables its author to win the post mortem while losing the rubber.

Blackwood
A convention employed by players who compensate for their inability to bid intelligently by proving that they can count up to four.

Pre-Emptive Bid
A bid intended to make it difficult for opponents, and impossible for partner, to play the contract.

Psychic Bid
A bid based on the dubious premise that opponents are more gullible than partner.

Relay Sequence
A means of increasing the number of bids needed to reach the wrong contract.

Splinter Bid
A bid enabling declarer to display expert trump control when playing in a one-nil fit.

Principle of Restricted Choice
The earth-shattering revelation that a defender who plays an honour under a higher one may do so because he has no option.

Percentage Play
A play invariably chosen by those experts who value pure mathematics above psychology, inference and table presence.

Opening Lead
The first vital lead, usually described as moronic if unsuccessful, or obvious if successful.

Grand Coup
A spectacular trump reducing play which occurs in reported hands daily, and at the table bicentennially.

Safety Play
A play which risks a contract against normal distribution by ensuring it against adverse distribution.

Misfit
A hand where partner's poor judgement prevents the contract being played in your suit.

Screens
An instrument of mercy, employed during the bidding to minimise the erosion of partnership confidence caused by expressions of mutual disgust.

Major Upset
The defeat of the unbeatable by the unspeakable.

Duplicate Bridge
A pernicious system of comparing results, which turns the suspicion that a player is bad into a certainty.

5
HEMINGWAY

In the nineteen-twenties and thirties, America exported jazz, contract bridge and a vast army of expatriate writers who were called 'The Lost Generation'. They lived mainly in Paris and, like Ernest Hemingway, worshipped drink, food, sex, lack of sex, and dangerous pastimes like bull-fighting, hunting and contract bridge.

Hemingway was his own greatest creation, tough, bold and boundlessly energetic. His mentor, Gertrude Stein, once said to her dog, "Be fierce. Act like Hemingway."

His writing was simple, apparently artless, and very direct. Had he played bridge, his bidding would have been full of massive pre-empts and death-defying overcalls. Yet there is a quaintness which is all his own in Hemingway's dialogue – his characters are constantly engaged in bilingual conversation, which both creates atmosphere and displays the author's linguistic prowess.

He was accused of being the original Limelight Kid; he was always where the action was. So if the first ever recorded double coup en passant was played in Paris in 1929, Ernest would have been there.

Paris in the Rain

On this morning I was walking in the *Rue de Rivoli* and it was raining. So I got sick of the rain and went into a cafe. I did not know why I did this. You just had to do what you did.

I ordered a *litre* of *vin du patron* and they had to hand it to me over a crowd that was four deep at the bar, drinking *Pernod* and laughing and singing.

I said, *"Excusez moi,"* and pushed past some *gendarmes*, and a group of men playing accordions and found an empty chair next to four people who were playing cards.

I sat down and one of the players looked at me and said, *"Mon dieu, c'est un Kibitzeur!"* and I knew their game was bridge.

An old man was frowning at his cards and the other three were drinking and smoking and I knew it must be the old man's lead. He pulled out cards and pushed them back and the girl on his right yawned and smiled at me.

"You are *Américain*," she said.

"Does it show?"

"I 'ave bid *le petit schlem* and the old fool cannot make the *décision* what to lead," she laughed.

"Slams can have that effect," I said.

"Do you 'ave an American *cigarette?*" she asked.

"Oui," I said fluently, and I 'anded her my pack and we smoked and drank while the *homme vieux* pulled out a card and pushed it back. Then he said, *"Que sera sera,"* and led the knave of clubs.

The girl's partner put down *le mort* and she looked at it and spat.

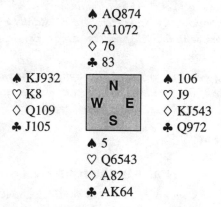

♠ AQ874
♥ A1072
♦ 76
♣ 83

♠ KJ932   ♠ 106
♥ K8   ♥ J9
♦ Q109   ♦ KJ543
♣ J105   ♣ Q972

♠ 5
♥ Q6543
♦ A82
♣ AK64

Contract 6♡ by *Sud*. The ♣J led.

She lit another *cigarette* and murmured *"Impossible!"* which I knew was French for impossible. There seemed no way to avoid two losers, a trump and a diamond.

She won in hand and took the spade *finesse*. She cross-ruffed the black suits and when East followed to the fourth club she said, *"Ah! Maintenant c'est possible!"* and somehow I knew that now it was possible.

These were the last four cards:

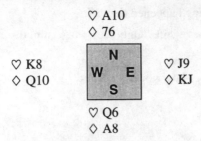

♡ A10
◊ 76

♡ K8   ♡ J9
◊ Q10   ◊ KJ

♡ Q6
◊ A8

"*Regardez!*" she said. "Until now, neither of my *adversaires* could ruff without the sacrifice of their *trompe* trick. And now, *mon ami*, for the *coup de grâce.*" She played the ◊ A and ◊ 8 and said, "*Voilà!*"

East won with the ◊ K and he said "*Merde!*" He led the ♡ J and the girl covered and the old man threw in his cards and said, "*Merde aussi!*"

I said, "*C'est magnifique!*" I wanted to say more but I did not know the French for coup en passant.

So I gave her another *cigarette* and she bought drinks with the *francs* she won with her *petit schlem* which was *vulnérable* and *redoublé.*

"You must come to America with me," I said.

"Why should I do that?"

"You could win a fortune at bridge."

"But you have *le Prohibition.*"

"But we still drink."

"Then why do you live in *Paris*?"

"I came here for the bullfights."

"They are in Spain."

"I am one of the Lost Generation."

"Oh, a writer." She spat. "*Paris* is full of them. What is your name?"

"F. Scott Dos Passos Wolfe."

"That a funny name."

"I was thinking of changing it."

"Would you like to make love to me?"

"I'm sorry. *C'est impossible.*"

"*Pourquoi?*"

"The war ... something happened to me."

"*Les Boches!*" She spat again. "Only they would aim there."

"True."

"This dialogue. It is ... how you say? Short?"

"Terse."

"Why should that be?"

"I get paid by the line."

We drank some more wine and smoked and waited until the rain stopped, and I said *au revoir* to the girl. She said I should write a story about her.

But I never did.

6

MIKE LAWRENCE

Mike Lawrence is one of the world's greatest players. A member of the original Dallas Aces, he has won two world championships and a string of victories in all the major American competitions.

His books How to Read Your Opponents' Cards *and* The Complete Book of Overcalls *have become standards in their own fields. He is an original thinker, with a lucid style. No decoration. No nonsense.*

One of his major contributions to bidding theory is advocating four card suit overcalls, especially when holding five cards of the opponent's suit. But there could be more to come from this fertile mind. Perhaps overcalls on three or even two cards suits? That could well be the subject of Lawrence's next book but one. For the uninitiated, RHO is a standard abbreviation for Right-Hand Opponent.

Overcalling On Short Suits

Overcalls on four card suits are now routine. But why not three card suits? Or even two card suits? Particularly at matchpoints. This is where bad bridge wins. I know. I've been there.

I like short suits almost as much as short sentences. But for different reasons. Short sentences are easy to read. But short suit overcalls are not easy to read. Let me show you some examples.

RHO opens one club. You hold:

♠ AQ10
♡ 5
♢ J86
♣ AJ9753

Bid one spade. Your length in clubs means partner will be short. Or even shorter. He is also likely to have spade support. The full hand was:

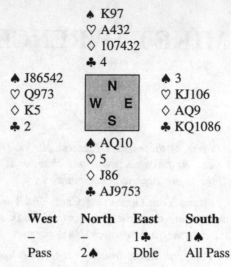

	♠ K97		
	♡ A432		
	◇ 107432		
	♣ 4		

West	North	East	South
–	–	1♣	1♠
Pass	2♠	Dble	All Pass

West led a club. [1]+670.

Now for two card overcalls. The requirements for these are more stringent. You need six cards in the opponent's suit. And good controls. An honour in your suit is preferable. But not essential.

Love All. Dealer East.

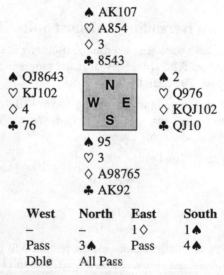

West	North	East	South
–	–	1◇	1♠
Pass	3♠	Pass	4♠
Dble	All Pass		

West led a diamond. [2]+590

You think two card overcalls are dangerous? *This* is dangerous:

RHO bids 1♡. You hold:

♠ KJ9732
♡ 2
♢ A105
♣ K43

Pass. An overcall could be risky. Your shortage in hearts marks partner with length. If he also has length in the minors you will run into a nasty penalty.

The full hand was:

North/South Game. Dealer East.

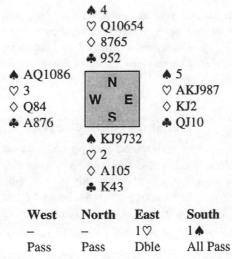

```
                    ♠ 4
                    ♡ Q10654
                    ♢ 8765
                    ♣ 952
  ♠ AQ1086                         ♠ 5
  ♡ 3                              ♡ AKJ987
  ♢ Q84                            ♢ KJ2
  ♣ A876                           ♣ QJ10
                    ♠ KJ9732
                    ♡ 2
                    ♢ A105
                    ♣ K43
```

West	North	East	South
–	–	1♡	1♠
Pass	Pass	Dble	All Pass

South was held to three tricks. A penalty of 1100.

I have been asked many times my opinion of overcalls on singletons. My answer is that the world is not ready for them. Yet . . . . But give short suit overcalls a try. You will get to be declarer more often. With a little fore-sight, partner need hardly ever play a hand. At least till he has read this article.

---

[1] See Mike Lawrence: *What to Lead When They Play In Your Six Card Suit.*
[2] It's amazing how many people have not read this book.

7
MY LIFE IN BRIDGE

Omar Sharif is probably the world's most famous bridge player. To many, this is the same as saying that Sir Francis Drake was its most famous bowls player. The difference is that, while nobody knows how Drake would have compared with David Bryant, we do know that Sharif is a first-class bridge player.

His book, Omar Sharif's Life in Bridge, *is part biography, part review of exciting hands he has been involved with. Some of them were for the Omar Sharif Circus, which was sponsored by Lancia in the seventies. Its members included Belladonna–Garozzo and Forquet–Sharif.*

The San Francisco Strip

Ely Culbertson always maintained that he had named his system bids 'approach' and 'forcing' because the courtship connotations would boost the sales of his books. Whether or not this is true, I have often thought that playing bridge is like making love to a beautiful woman. It may also be like making love to an ugly woman, but I am not in a position to say.

I was reminded of this analogy by a hand I played some years ago in America. When I returned to my hotel, I had found, waiting in my bed, the inevitable young woman who had broken into my room, armed with a revolver. It took me several hours to disarm and evict her and I wondered whether in future I should take the precaution of locking my door.

I was playing for the Omar Sharif Circus against those great rivals of the Dallas Aces, the San Francisco Queens. Our sponsors, Lancia, always gave six cars to any team who beat us, and we had just received a letter from the managing director thanking us for our efforts in helping them to double their production.

The match was a tight one, and by the final board I sensed that it could go either way. I was South and found myself in an awkward contract of 6♣.

Game All. Dealer South.

♠ J83
♡ KQ103
◇ J76
♣ K95

♠ A762
♡ AJ6
◇ A
♣ AQJ104

West	North	East	South
–	–	–	1♣
1NT(i)	Dble	3◇	4♣
Pass	5♣	Pass	6♣
All Pass			

(i) Spades and diamonds or hearts and clubs

West led a rather cautious ♣8 and I think you will agree that prospects looked rather bleak. A squeeze against West seemed to depend on his holding the ♠KQ and the ◇KQ which was rather a lot to hope for. I could sense that my opponents were already anticipating the big prize. They were looking at me and exchanging delighted glances. I hoped they were thinking of the six Lancias!

I took the lead in hand and sipped my Dom Perignon as I reviewed the options. Somehow my thoughts went back to that terrifying encounter of the previous night and suddenly the solution was staring me in the face. A strip tease!

No, not a stratagem to disorientate the delightful gentlemen on my left, but a method of squeezing him to the appropriate shape for an end-play, though I thought it prudent not to tell him so. As long as he held the ♠KQ the contract was makeable.

I ran off clubs and hearts, reaching the following position:

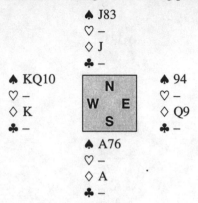

<pre>
              ♠ J83
              ♡ –
              ◇ J
              ♣ –
  ♠ KQ10   ┌───────┐   ♠ 94
  ♡ –   │   N   │   ♡ –
  ◇ K   │ W   E │   ◇ Q9
  ♣ –   │   S   │   ♣ –
            └───────┘
              ♠ A76
              ♡ –
              ◇ A
              ♣ –
</pre>

You can see it was essential to squeeze West down to a singleton diamond before playing the ◇ A. It was now a simple matter to cash that card and lead a spade towards dummy.

The full hand was:

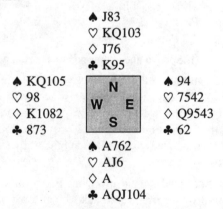

<pre>
               ♠ J83
               ♡ KQ103
               ◇ J76
               ♣ K95
  ♠ KQ105   ┌───────┐   ♠ 94
  ♡ 98   │   N   │   ♡ 7542
  ◇ K1082   │ W   E │   ◇ Q9543
  ♣ 873   │   S   │   ♣ 62
             └───────┘
               ♠ A762
               ♡ AJ6
               ◇ A
               ♣ AQJ104
</pre>

This hand gave me more pleasure than any of my achievements in the cinema. Even my most insignificant bridge trophies are displayed with pride. Those which I receive for my films are collecting dust in dark corners.

The British writer, Denis Spooner, once said that when he saw *Lawrence of Arabia* and I first appeared as a distant mounted figure charging towards my jealously guarded waterhole, he expected me, having shot the intruder, to leap off my camel, walk up to Peter O'Toole and say, "You hold: five spades to the ace-queen, six hearts to the king , . . ."
If only I had thought of it at the time.

8

A STUDY IN SHERLOCK

The Sherlock Holmes Hotel in Baker Street once had a manager called Holmes. So many people used to ask him if he was a descendant of the great detective that he eventually gave up denying the fact. He then became so weary of being asked to locate lost pets and jewellery that he sought refuge as a domestic bursar at Cambridge, where he is now asked by the professors to search for lost manuscripts.

Holmes became so real that Conan Doyle killed him off, but some years later he was forced by public demand to bring him back to life, and he certainly lived through the golden age of contract. His maxim, "eliminate the impossible and whatever remains, however improbable, is the truth," is quite a good description of how to analyse a difficult hand.

Holmes referred to London as "that great city". Conan Doyle called it "that great cesspool into which all loungers of Europe are irresistibly drained".

Murder at the Regency Club

"Watson, kindly read this and tell me what you deduce?"

Holmes passed me a letter which I peered at through the dense clouds of pipe smoke. To allow me to concentrate, he mercifully stopped playing his violin.

"It is from someone called James Frobisher," I said. "He wishes to consult you and intends to call at noon today."

"Nothing more?"

"Only that he uses the stationery of the Regency Club."

"Really, Watson? Yet I think we can conclude that he is rich, intelligent and a keen bridge player."

"Astounding, Holmes."

"Elementary, Watson. His intellect is manifested in his style and penmanship. Only the rich can afford membership of London's most exclusive gaming club."

"But why bridge?" I protested. "The Regency has every game imaginable."

He smiled. "None but the king of card games could provide the mental challenge craved by the writer of that letter."

He took it to the window and held it up in the sunlight. "We can also surmise that our client is tall, slim and heavily bearded."

"Holmes you surpass yourself!"

"Not at all, Watson. It is one minute to twelve and I can see him at our front door. I had better put away my violin."

"I agree, Holmes. He may be a music lover."

Our visitor was an impressive man, who believed in dispensing with formalities. "Yesterday gentlemen, I was at the club, having just gone down in a vulnerable four spades, when an anonymous note was delivered to the table. It threatened that unless I paid twenty thousand pounds I would die in a manner too awful to contemplate."

"Tell me about it," said Holmes.

"I held five spades to the ace-king-eight ...."

"No, Mr. Frobisher," I interrupted him, "My friend does not mean ...."

"You are mistaken Watson. The hand may have some bearing on the case."

Frobisher produced a notebook and wrote the following:

Game All. Dealer East.

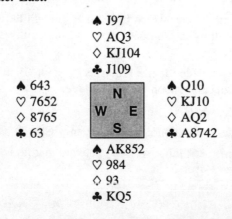

```
                    ♠ J97
                    ♡ AQ3
                    ◇ KJ104
                    ♣ J109
    ♠ 643                          ♠ Q10
    ♡ 7652          N              ♡ KJ10
    ◇ 8765       W     E           ◇ AQ2
    ♣ 63            S              ♣ A8742
                    ♠ AK852
                    ♡ 984
                    ◇ 93
                    ♣ KQ5
```

West	North	East	South
–	–	1♣	1♠
Pass	3♠	Pass	4♠
All Pass			

"West led the ♣6. East won and returned a club, which I took in hand. As the cards lie, you can see that the contract is, I believe you would say, elementary."

"I agree," said Holmes. "After drawing trumps, carefully unblocking the nine and the knave, you should run the ◇9. East wins and can do no better than play a club which you take in hand. You knock out the ◇A and ruff the next club lead. Dummy's two winning diamonds give you your ten tricks."

Frobisher sighed. "But on the first round of trumps, East dropped the queen! I finessed West for the ten, but East won and gave his partner a club ruff. West led a heart; I stupidly played the queen. Gentlemen, I lost a spade, two clubs, two diamonds and two hearts. An ignominious four down."

Holmes relit his pipe and the room began to darken, "You yielded to temptation unnecessarily. And now I have a deduction and a question. First the deduction. East, who engineered that cunning defence, was that master of deception, Professor Moriarty."

"Holmes!"

"It is typical not only of his play, gentlemen, but his brazen effrontery. Who but he would contrive to be present to gloat over his intended victim? I have long suspected that he is behind the wave of extortion that befouls our great city."

"The villain!" one of us cried; I forgot who.

"And now for my question," said Holmes, turning ominously to our guest. "What have you done with the real James Frobisher?"

"I do not understand you."

"When you wrote those bridge hands I noticed that in an otherwise competent forgery, your capital As differed from those in Frobisher's letter. Don't move – *Professor!*"

I realised to my horror that we were facing the notorious Moriarty, the Napoleon of crime. He sat perfectly still, sneering arrogantly.

"Very wise," said Holmes. "Under the cover of my tobacco smoke I have a Smith & Weston pointed at your dolichocephalic skull, with its unique supra-orbital development. That was one feature you could not disguise, Professor. Now, where is Frobisher?"

"Where you will never find him."

"And why did you come here in his stead?"

"To put an end to a life which has become a nuisance to me."

"You forget, Professor, that it is my revolver which is aimed at you."

"You meddling fool! Did you think I came unprepared? In my hand is a powerful grenade. Should you shoot, my grip will relax and we will be blown to pieces."

My old friend was in danger. Swift action was called for.

"Stay there Holmes," I said. "I will go for help."

"There is no need, Doctor," said Moriarty. "I am leaving, and you can do nothing to stop me. Au revoir, Mr. Holmes, for we shall assuredly meet again."

"Until that time," said Holmes, "I suggest that you reflect on the deficiencies of your defence."

(The hand is repeated for convenience)

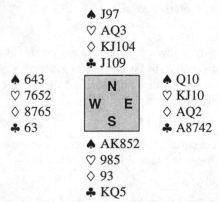

```
                    ♠ J97
                    ♡ AQ3
                    ◇ KJ104
                    ♣ J109
   ♠ 643          ┌─────────┐        ♠ Q10
   ♡ 7652         │    N    │        ♡ KJ10
   ◇ 8765         │ W     E │        ◇ AQ2
   ♣ 63           │    S    │        ♣ A8742
                  └─────────┘
                    ♠ AK852
                    ♡ 985
                    ◇ 93
                    ♣ KQ5
```

"It was a deceptive masterpiece, years ahead of its time," said Moriarty.

"You think so? Frobisher should have rejected the putative finesse. It was obvious that had the queen of spades been a singleton there would have been no play for the contract."

Moriarty laughed mirthlessly. "But I gave him the opportunity to play badly, and he gripped it with both hands, his and dummy's."

"An alternative strategy would be for you to have played well."

Moriarty turned white with fury. "Are you suggesting that I did not do so?"

"At trick two, you should have led a heart. Constantly profiting from the weakness of others, you are often apt to overlook your own."

Moriarty's malevolence was almost tangible. Still clutching the grenade, he backed through the door and was lost in the milling throng of Baker Street.

"A stalemate, Holmes," I remarked, emerging from behind the chaise longue.

"No Watson, we won the first round. When he realises the correctness of the heart switch, his self confidence will be shattered irretrievably."

"But Holmes, to lead away from a king, round to dummy's tenace ... it is the play of a beginner."

"Or a master. It is essential if the defence is to create a heart trick before declarer can establish his diamonds. I recommend that you study the hand at your leisure."

"We have no time, Holmes. We must rescue the real Frobisher."

He took out his violin. "No, Watson. I am afraid that a man who can murder a contract as he did is scarcely worth saving."

9
BLIND BRIDGE DATE

It is interesting to try and imagine the first presentation of the idea for this famous TV show to the heads of programme selection:

To Head of Light Entertaiment From Ivor Winner

FORMAT FOR NEW TYPE OF GAME SHOW

1. Star introduces three young women to studio audience.
2. Young man enters, hidden from young women by screen. Star introduces him to studio audience.
3. Young man puts questions to each of the young women in turn.
   - 3.1 Their answers, like the questions, are designed by the programme's scriptwriters.
   - 3.2 None of the studio audience guesses this.
4. The young man chooses for his blind date the young woman who has the best scriptwriter.
5. They go on the blind date.
6. They come back the following week and we see film of them learning to water-ski, ride horses, etc.
   - 6.1 They keep falling off.
7. The star asks them how they got on and they both say they couldn't stand each other.

Yet the show has been phenomenally successful, and it could have all sorts of intriguing spin-offs. So why not Blind Bridge Date, for all the people who are still searching for their ideal bridge partner?

And of course the star would be the incomparable Cilla Black ....

Ron and Elsie in Paris

Cilla: Now that we've met our three lovely young ladies, let's meet the young man who wants to play Blind Date. His name's Ron and he's from Surbiton.

(Applause: Ron enters)

Hello, Ron.

Ron: Hello, Cilla.

Cilla: Tell us about yourself, Ron.

Ron: I'm a national master and I play Acol with Benjamin two bids.

Cilla: Oh. good. I like Benjy two bids myself.

Ron: So do I, Cilla.

Cilla: I know you do, Ron, otherwise you wouldn't play them, would you? Now tell me your idea of the perfect bridge partner.

Ron: I think Benito Garozzo.

Cilla: Well we haven't got her, but we have got three smashing, gorgeous partners for you to choose from. So let's have your first question.

Ron: My first question is: if you were my partner and your opening one no trump was doubled, what action would you take over my redouble? Number one please?

Number 1: Well Ron, if you were to pick me for your bridge date, I'd promise you all the action you could wish for.

Audience: Ooh!

Ron: Number two please?

Number 2: If I were lucky enough to be your partner, Ron, I'd want to leave it in.

Cilla: I think our Ron's going all hot under the collar.

Ron: Number three please?

Number 3: It would depend on the meaning of your redouble. Is it SOS or business?

Cilla: She sounds a deep one, doesn't she?

Ron: Yes, yes she does, Cilla. My second question is: under what circumstances would you regard my pass as forcing?

Number 1: Ron, I guarantee that, if we go on that bridge week, I'll regard all your passes as unconditionally forcing.

Ron: Number two?

Number 2: You wouldn't have to make any forcing passes, Ron. I'd be making enough for both of us.

Ron: Thank you. Number three?

Number 3: I'd regard a pass as forcing when the hand clearly belongs to us, or when there's a choice of doubling or ...

Cilla: All right number three. Ron's got his third question to ask.

Ron: My third question is: as declarer, under what circumstances do you duck twice? Number one?

Number 1: I'd duck whenever you asked me to, darling.

Ron: I see, number two?

Number 2: I don't know what a duck is, Ron, but you'll find I'm a very fast learner.

Ron: And number three?

Number 3: I duck twice when I have to lose the lead twice to establish my longest suit, or to ...

Cilla: Yes, number three. Now, Ron you've a very difficult choice to make and to help you make it, let's hear from our sexy mystery voice.

Voice: *Should he choose number one for some all action ducking? Or should he accept fast learning number two's offer to leave it in while she makes forcing passes? Or should he go with number three and spend the week-end playing bridge?*

Cilla: Oh, I bet it's a hard choice, Chuck?

Ron: It is, Cilla, but I'm going for number three.

Cilla: Ron, you've turned down two lovely, passionate ladies. How could you?

(The ladies are dismissed)

Now let's meet your Blind Bridge Date. She's Elsie from Birmingham.

(The screen slides back and Ron and Elsie are face to face.)

Now who'd like to choose the envelope?

Ron: I'll leave it to you, Elsie.

Elsie: It's a tournament in Paris!

Cilla: Oh, you'll love it! You'll be going up the Eiffel Tower, down the Seine by moonlight. You'll have lunch at Maxim's ...

Elsie: But what about the bridge?

Cilla: And you're going to have mixed pairs at Fontainebleu. Ooh, you'll love these, they're my favourite food. Now will you come back next week and tell us how you got on?

Ron: We certainly will, Cilla.

Elsie: Provided we finish in the top twenty.

(Ron and Elsie exit)

TRANSCRIPT OF FILM OF ELSIE AND RON AT MAXIM'S

Elsie: Now what shall we play over le Club Fort?

Ron: Double for majors.

Elsie: Oui. Et un sans `a tout pour les minors.

Ron: And weak jump overcalls?

Waiter: Champagne, mademoiselle?

Elsie: Non, merci, garçon.

Waiter: C'est Bollinger, mademoiselle.

Elsie: Et Bollinger `a vous. Ce soir, nous jouons le pont.

Ron: Elsie, it's not le pont, it's le bridge. And the future tense of jouer is ...

Elsie: Sputniks to three spades?

TRANSCRIPT ALTERNATING BETWEEN ELSIE AND RON

Ron: Our system discussions were OK. But when it came down to it, she just hogged all the contracts.

CUT TO ...

Elsie: His dummy play was awful. So I decided to play everything. That's why we rose from thirty-fourth to ninth.

CUT TO ...

Ron: We were always playing against the room. Otherwise we'd have finished in the top six.

CUT TO ...

Elsie: I'd play with him again, but only if he came to Birmingham.

CUT TO ...

Ron: I'd play with her again, but she'd have to come to London.

TRANSCRIPT OF FINAL INTERVIEW WITH CILLA

Cilla: Oh, what a pity. I had such high hopes for you.

Elsie: Cilla, he held ♠Q10932 ♡A10986 ◇432 ♣–. I opened 1♠, and do you know what he did?

Cilla: No, but I'm sure you'll tell me, Elsie.

Elsie: He raised to 4♠. With two first round controls!

Cilla: He didn't!

Elsie: So I passed and we made six. Would you travel a hundred miles just to miss laydown slams? And how about this?

(Camera focuses on bridge hand)

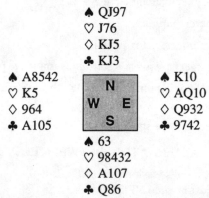

```
              ♠ QJ97
              ♡ J76
              ◇ KJ5
              ♣ KJ3
  ♠ A8542                    ♠ K10
  ♡ K5          N            ♡ AQ10
  ◇ 964      W     E         ◇ Q932
  ♣ A105        S            ♣ 9742
              ♠ 63
              ♡ 98432
              ◇ A107
              ♣ Q86
```

Elsie: South was in one no trump. North had opened one spade. Ron led the ♡K.

Ron: And what did you do? You only overtook with the ♡A! And what did you lead back? The bloody ◇2. Round to dummy's ◇KJ.

Audience:	Oooh!
	(They are clearly shocked at Elsie's violation of the principle of leading through strength and up to weakness.)
Elsie:	Because, Pudding Head, after your crackpot lead, declarer was virtually certain to be 2-5-3-3.
Ron:	So?
Elsie:	So we had to attack a minor. If you had the ♢A, my switch would have beaten it by two.
Ron:	But I didn't have the ♢A, did I?
Elsie:	But all you had to do was follow my defence and it would still have been one off. We take two spades, three hearts one diamond and a club. And we would still have done, except for you.
Cilla:	What did he do, Elsie?
Elsie:	When he was in with the ♣A, he just led the ♡5, setting up declarer's suit.
Ron:	See what I mean? She keeps telling me what to do, and she's not even a regional master.
Cilla:	Well I'm sorry, Ron. It seems you'll have to try and get Miss Benita Garozzo after all. But now it's time to meet three young men who want to play Blind Chess Date.

10
SKID

'Skid' – S.J. Simon – was a great bridge player and one of the pioneers of the Acol system. His book, Why you lose at Bridge is one of the cornerstones of the game's literature.

He was a charismatic, amusing, myopic, pot-bellied, untidy chainsmoker. But as Guy Ramsey said, like John Wilkes he was only a quarter of an hour behind the handsomest man in London. He was also the co-author, with Caryl Brahms, of a series of inspired humorous novels, beginning with Bullet in the Ballet.

One of his most famous contributions to bridge was the 'Masterbid'. As South, you hold:

♠ 953
♡ K7
◇ 6543
♣ 7432

and the bidding goes:

West	North	East	South
–	–	1♣	Pass
1◇	2♣	2◇	Pass
3♣	3◇	4◇	Pass
Pass	5♣	Pass	5◇
Pass	6♠	Pass	?

South's masterbid is 7♠.

Skid created four memorable characters; the Unlucky Expert, whose brilliance was offset by his inability to handle inferior partners, like Mrs Guggenheim, who practically invented the crime of 'contracticide', Futile Willy, who knew everything about bridge except how to win, and Mr Smug, with his touching delusions of adequacy.

Why I Win at Bridge

Bridge used to be a simple game. Until the scientists took over. They started a plague of asking bids, relay bids, transfer bids, unamusing cue bids, waiting bids, and, the final horror, multi-coloured bids. Please don't misunderstand me; some scientists are among my favourite people. They are also my favourite opponents. They chuck thousands of points every time they sit down to play.

Thousands!

Only yesterday I watched two internationals take eight bids to reach two hearts redoubled. On a one-one trump fit! They went five down.

And they were lucky. The adverse trumps broke six-five.

I'll never forget the time Harrison Gray and I were asked by two super scientists how we managed to reach three no trumps on Board 14 of the National Pairs. Our complicated sequence, with notes for the benefit of the scientists, went like this:

> North (Simon)   1NT   (i)
> South (Gray)   3NT   (ii)
>
> (i) I have a one no trump opening
> (ii) In that case I think we can make three.

It so happened that we each had a doubleton club and the defence took the first five tricks, but, with no opposition bidding to help him, East revoked, giving us a cold top.

Keep your bidding simple. Imagine your partner is somebody's old maiden aunt from Basingstoke with a bag of knitting and an ear trumpet. And bid what she will understand.

If we can state the commonest source of bidding chucks, we will have won half the battle. To my mind they are:

No trump bidding	Underbidding small hands
Suit bidding	Underbidding big hands
Contested auctions	Overbidding small hands
Uncontested auctions	Slam bidding
Overbidding big hands	Sacrifice bidding

So, if we can tidy up these areas, we'll have nothing left to worry about. Let's start with no trump bidding.

Imagine you hold:

♠ AKJ32
♡ 753
◇ AQ106
♣ 2

You bid one spade, partner responds two clubs. You rebid two diamonds. Partner bids two hearts.

Don't deny it. You are tempted to bid two no trumps. Or even three. Go on, admit it. I promise I won't tell anyone.

To my mind, the only bid is pass. Yes, I know it means giving up all that modern rubbish like change of suit forcing and fourth suit forcing, but forget it. It takes away all partner's natural bids.

He might hold:

♠ 5
♡ A986
◇ 874
♣ AK1084

And even if you only bid two no trumps, on that hand he will raise you to three. Of course you will make it. Once in a month of Sundays, with every card right and a bit of help from the defence.

Two hearts is a nice safe resting place. What a pity the super scientists have condemned it as Unfit for Habitation.

The next abomination I want to destroy forever is the Transfer Bid. Why? You'll see why when you look at this hand from a match.

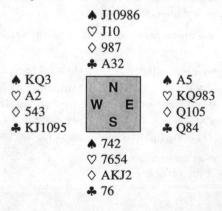

```
              ♠ J10986
              ♡ J10
              ◇ 987
              ♣ A32
♠ KQ3                        ♠ A5
♡ A2          N             ♡ KQ983
◇ 543      W     E          ◇ Q105
♣ KJ1095      S             ♣ Q84
              ♠ 742
              ♡ 7654
              ◇ AKJ2
              ♣ 76
```

The bidding in Room One went like this:

West	North	East	South
1NT	Pass	2◊(i)	Dble
Pass	Pass	3NT(ii)	All Pass

(i) Transfer to hearts
(ii) Pushy, but what else?

North's ◊ 9 was a killing lead. One down!

The bidding in the other room was different:

West	North	East	South
1NT	Pass	3♡	Pass
3NT	All Pass		

This time North led the ♠J. Declarer put up dummy's ♠A, crossed to the ♡A and led a small club. North played low! He turned out to be wrong, but can you really blame him?

I hope not. Because I was North.

Having disposed of Transfer Bids, I am going to train my big guns on Stayman, the most over-used convention since Blackwood. And I'll get to him later.

West		East
♠ AQ42		♠ KJ75
♡ K9		♡ A10
◊ QJ10		◊ A942
♣ Q932		♣ J107

Three no trumps is cold on any distribution. It should be bid:

West	East	
1NT	3NT	*(West is the old lady with the ear trumpet)*

But how do you think it was bid in that same team of four? You've guessed it:

West	East
1NT	2♣
2♠	4♠

The defence was really expert. The ♣AK and a club ruff. Then cunningly South waited to make his ◊ K.

Now I want to deal with the latest horror that is creeping into bridge and which must be stopped before it takes hold. The Unusual No Trump. This hand will show you why:

North/South Game. Dealer South.

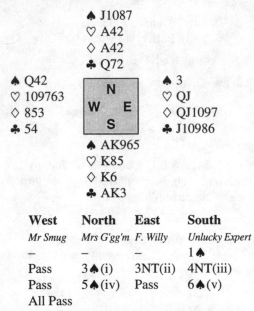

```
                    ♠ J1087
                    ♡ A42
                    ◇ A42
                    ♣ Q72
   ♠ Q42          ┌─────────┐        ♠ 3
   ♡ 109763       │    N    │        ♡ QJ
   ◇ 853          │ W     E │        ◇ QJ1097
   ♣ 54           │    S    │        ♣ J10986
                  └─────────┘
                    ♠ AK965
                    ♡ K85
                    ◇ K6
                    ♣ AK3
```

West	North	East	South
Mr Smug	*Mrs G'gg'm*	*F. Willy*	*Unlucky Expert*
–	–	–	1♠
Pass	3♠(i)	3NT(ii)	4NT(iii)
Pass	5♠(iv)	Pass	6♠(v)
All Pass			

(i)   Mrs Guggenheim makes her first good bid of the week

(ii) A typical Futile Willy lunacy

(iii) A dubious bid. Mrs Guggenheim is not in the same class as the lady with the ear trumpet. She never remembers Blackwood.

(iv) She doesn't. She shows three aces.

(v)   A test for the Unlucky Expert's ethics, but he bids the slam. He has to, his side has five aces!

Mr Smug led the ◇5 and the Unlucky Expert took stock. He reasoned that Futile Willy must hold two six-card minors, so that West was likely to have the ♠Q twice-guarded, in which case there was no legitimate play for the contract. So he took the opening lead in hand and at trick two he smoothly led the ♠5.

Mr Smug was too old a hand to fall for a trick like that. He had seen defenders' honours crashed before. So he smugly played low! Declarer won with the ♠J and made twelve tricks.

Whether the Unlucky Expert was for once lucky, or Mr Smug played badly is beside the point. But for Futile Willy's atrocious bid of 3NT, declarer would certainly have laid down the ♠AK for one down.

Another modern abomination which I personally abominate is the Weak Jump Overcall. I call it, 'sending a boy on a man's errand'. I don't know what you call it, but I hope it's something equally vitriolic.

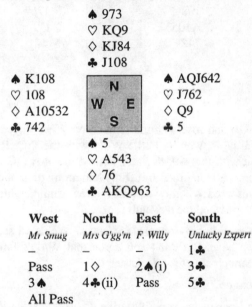

```
              ♠ 973
              ♡ KQ9
              ◇ KJ84
              ♣ J108
♠ K108                        ♠ AQJ642
♡ 108                         ♡ J762
◇ A10532                      ◇ Q9
♣ 742                         ♣ 5
              ♠ 5
              ♡ A543
              ◇ 76
              ♣ AKQ963
```

West	North	East	South
Mr Smug	Mrs G'gg'm	F. Willy	Unlucky Expert
–	–	–	1♣
Pass	1◇	2♠(i)	3♣
3♠	4♣(ii)	Pass	5♣
All Pass			

(i) Aren't you glad you don't have a Futile Willy for a partner? This bid shows six spades and 6-9 points.

(ii) Mrs Guggenheim always raises partner at the drop of a hat. She knows that being dummy is the best part of her game.

Mr Smug led the ♠K. You don't like it? Neither do I, but that's what he did. He followed with the ♠10, ruffed by declarer. The Unlucky Expert could now place the ◇A with West, since Futile Willy would have felt he was losing face if he made a jump overcall with a decent hand. However, there was the question of what to do with the fourth heart. If either clubs were 2-2, or hearts 3-3, the contract was on ice, but the Unlucky Expert could see a way of coping when, as seemed likely after Willy's futile intervention, neither suit broke.

(The hand is repeated for convenience.)

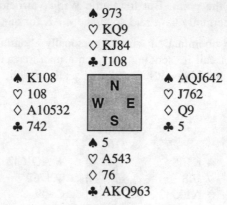

```
              ♠ 973
              ♡ KQ9
              ◇ KJ84
              ♣ J108
♠ K108                        ♠ AQJ642
♡ 108          N              ♡ J762
◇ A10532    W     E           ◇ Q9
♣ 742          S              ♣ 5
              ♠ 5
              ♡ A543
              ◇ 76
              ♣ AKQ963
```

He led the ◇6 and rose with the king when West played low. He played the ◇4 from table, won by Futile Willy with the ◇Q. Ruffing the spade continuation with the ♣9, declarer cashed the ♣A and crossed twice to dummy's top hearts in order to ruff his remaining diamonds high. Now his carefully preserved ♣3 allowed him to draw trumps with dummy's ♣J10 and the ♡A provided the eleventh trick.

So it was a neat dummy reversal. So what? We've all seem them before. Certainly we have. But don't you agree that Willy's fatuous call of 2♠ made it that much easier for declarer?

Of course you do.

Well? Have I persuaded you all to give up all that scientific nonsense and bid simply naturally? I have? Good! Then I will welcome you to my club any time. You'll chuck thousands at me.

Thousands!

11
TOPS AND BOTTOMS

Matthew Granovetter is one of America's leading players. He is also a lyricist and composer, whose superb card-play is occasionally conducted at the tempo of a funeral march. Matthew and his wife, Pamela, asked 100 world class players to submit favourite deals and they published 52 of them in Tops and Bottoms. The hands were described by at least two experts as the greatest they had ever seen.

The format of the book is that after the play of each hand is reviewed the co-authors hold a post-mortem in an entertaining dialogue. Just occasionally, the exchanges look as if they might become a little peppery, but they never quite do so.

However, there is a devil in all of us.

Devil's Coup

Matthew:	The time is 1933. Harry, a victim of the Depression, is about to jump off Brooklyn Bridge, when a dark, handsome stranger appears from nowhere.
Pamela:	Was it you darling?
Matthew:	I wasn't around in 1933. And I didn't say he was that handsome. But he did make Harry a handsome offer. Twenty years of phenomenal luck, at a price of course.
Pamela:	His soul.
Matthew:	You know the story?
Pamela:	I've read Marlowe and Goethe and Benet.
Matthew:	Well, this one is by Sidney Lenz.
Pamela:	Is this a parody about him or us?

Matthew: Both. Anyway, Harry signs the standard infernal agreement
             and enjoys every happiness in the world. Until, twenty years
             later to the second, the stranger, whose name was B.L.
             Zebub, appears in a puff of smoke to exact payment.

Pamela: Wasn't there an escape clause?

Matthew: Yes. Zebub offers to flip a coin, but what chance does Harry
             have against a master of tele ...

Pamela: Kinesis.

Matthew: Just then, Harry's wife Dorothy arrives. She is a gorgeous
             blonde, who is a curly wolf at bridge and never finishes her
             husband's sentences. She shows them a hand her partner had
             misplayed that afternoon.

                         ♠ AJ87
                         ♡ –
                         ◇ AKQJ
                         ♣ AJ1043

    ♠ Q95   ♠ K6432
    ♡ 32   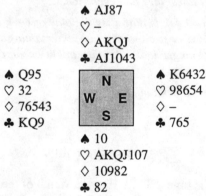   ♡ 98654
    ◇ 76543   ◇ –
    ♣ KQ9   ♣ 765

                         ♠ 10
                         ♡ AKQJ107
                         ◇ 10982
                         ♣ 82

Game All. Dealer North.

West	North	East	South
–	1♣	1♠	3♡
Pass	6NT	Pass	7♡
All Pass			

Pamela: A typical, everyday humdrum deal. But that bidding! And
             why didn't East double for an unusual lead?

Matthew: This was 1933. A double would have asked partner to lead
             the suit first bid by dummy. Well, Zebub maintains that 7♡
             is unmakeable, even with the ♠Q lead. Dorothy bets she can
             make it against any defence. Harry's soul depends upon the
             outcome. Over to you Pamela.

Pamela: I cover the ♠Q with the ♠A. I lead the ♠J, East has to cover, so I ruff in hand. I've transferred the menace to West.

Matthew: You're not supposed to say things like that. You're supposed to say, "Gee, Matt, honey, what should I do next?"

Pamela: Am I? Well I'm sick of being low man on your frigging totem pole. I'm co-author and now I'm going to play the ♡AKQJ10 and squeeze West's nuts off. And I didn't need a two-hour trance to work that out.

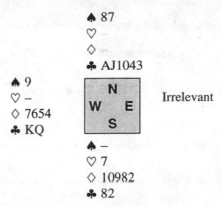

```
                    ♠ 87
                    ♡
                    ◊
                    ♣ AJ1043
      ♠ 9                              
      ♡ –            N                  Irrelevant
      ◊ 7654      W     E
      ♣ KQ            S
                    ♠ –
                    ♡ 7
                    ◊ 10982
                    ♣ 82
```

When the ♡7 is led, West is sunk without trace. I told you it was a plain, everyday hand. But wasn't it wonderful of Dorothy to save Harry's soul like that?

Matthew: She didn't. She overlooked the plain, everyday unblock. She got locked in dummy and poor Harry got whisked away to hell, leaving her with a broken heart and only $10,000,000 and her six lovers to console her.

Pamela: What a sad story. It doesn't sound like Sidney Lenz.

Matthew: Well maybe I improved it somewhat.

Pamela: Incidentally darling, what will I inherit if you ever go to that Great Bridge Club in the Sky?

Matthew: A massive overdraft. I'm a percentage player. I want to be sure that if ever I'm in the same position as Harry, you'll see no percentage in forgetting to unblock.

Pamela: As if I would! By the way, there's another story about the devil and a bridge player. He appeared before a famous expert and promised him he would win all the major tournaments and the World Championship three years running.

Matthew: Sounds interesting. And the price?

Pamela: His soul. his wife's soul, his children's souls and his grandchildren's souls.

Matthew: And what was the expert's reaction?

Pamela: He thought for a minute and said, "What's the catch?"

12
GRAND MASTER JEEVES

The servant who is in every way superior to his master appeared frequently in fiction long before P.G. Wodehouse created Jeeves. But Jeeves was the ultimate menial superman, and it is quite in character for him to reveal the fact that he is a bridge master when Bertie Wooster is in urgent need of one. He is known to have been a leading player at the Diogenes Club, an elite establishment for superior butlers and valets, and a repository for confidential information about their employers.

Everybody should have a Jeeves. Just imagine being able to summon a gin-sling bearing oracle and saying, "Jeeves, I need a quotation to introduce a humorous piece on bridge."

The reply might be something like: "May I suggest sir, that a particularly apt choice would be those lines of Garrick:

'Cards were first for benefit designed,
Sent to amuse, not to enslave the mind'

Or, if introducing a trump coup, sir, one might choose Cervantes:

'As much is lost by a card too many as a card too few'

I trust I have been of service, sir."

Your Lead, Jeeves

"Jeeves, I need to bend your ear."

"Yes, sir."

"You enjoyed your trip to Margate?"

"Most salubrious, sir."

"Did you consume oodles of fish?"

"It was my preferred diet, sir."

"Then can I take it that that gigantic brain of yours is in the absolute pink?"

"I shall endeavour to give satisfaction, sir."

But half a jiffy. I'm forgetting that my readers haven't the foggiest about my betrothal to Margot Latimer, so I'd better give you a run down.

If you picked someone to be marooned on the proverbial desert island with, Greta Garbo might be top of your list, but Margot wouldn't be more than a nose behind. She was moulded on the lines of Claudette Colbert, and it made the old corpuscles race just to cast an optic in her direction.

"Jeeves, it's about the Honourable Margot."

"I had anticipated that possibility, sir."

"She's been bitten by the bridge bug."

"Am I to conclude that she has fallen under the posthumous spell of Isambard Kingdom Brunel, sir, or could it be Mr Ely Culbertson?"

I gaped. That's all you can do when confounded by a massive intellect like that. Gape.

"Actually, Jeeves, I don't know either of the fellows. Bridge players, are they?"

"One of them, sir."

"Well the Hon. Lat. has told me she won't go ahead with the jolly old nuptials until I become a bridge expert."

"It could be a very long engagement, sir."

"What would you suggest?"

"That depends on your present level of attainment, sir."

"I've played the odd rubber with Aunt Dahlia."

"Are you familiar, sir, with the Milton Work point count?"

"Er no."

"The rule of eleven?"

"You've stumped me there, Jeeves."

"Could you possibly recall, sir, which are the major suits?"

I brightened. "Spades and hearts, Jeeves."

"Excellent, sir, You are already an automatic choice for the Drones' first team. If you will excuse me, sir?" He shimmered out and, moments later, shimmered in again, carrying three books.

"I recommend that you begin with this one, sir."

"You mean read it, Jeeves?"

"That would acknowledge its primary function, sir."

"It looks dashed difficult."

"I shall be continually at your side, sir. To elucidate."

I must say when Jeeves uses words like that it gives a fellow confidence. I flicked through the pages while he drifted off to brew a pot of Darjeeling.

Then I noticed the title, *Bridge for Beginners*. I bristled. The Wooster blood was definitely up. A man who can name both major suits without hesitation is not to be branded a beginner. I picked up another. It was called *Bridge for the Advancing Player*, and that's what I intended to do, advance.

I opened it at random and saw the following:

> ♠ K765
> ♡ K6
> ◇ A8
> ♣ A8754

> ♠ A8
> ♡ Q75
> ◇ KJ7543
> ♣ K6

Contract 3NT by South. The ♡ 4 led.

It didn't take me long to work out who South was. He was the chap with all those diamonds. I did a spot of pondering and suddenly the solution hit me.

The other hand was dummy!

I lit a pleased cigarette. By the time Jeeves returned I was well into the second part of the problem, which seemed to be the small matter of making three no trumps. Jeeves gave one of his discreet coughs.

"I see you have finished the first book I recommended, sir, and are well into the third."

"It's easy when you get the hang of it, Jeeves. Take this hand. I play low from dummy.

"Really, sir? East is unlikely to play the ace and when you take with your queen, the heart suit, in vulgar parlance, is wide open. I recommend playing the king from dummy, sir. We will assume it holds. How would you proceed, sir."

"I'd reel off all those jolly looking diamonds, Jeeves."

"A strategy worthy of von Clausewitz, sir. May I ask how?"

"How Jeeves? I don't understand. When you reel, you reel."

"An intermediate player would lead the ace and finesse the jack, sir."

"That's what I meant, Jeeves. I'd reel with finesse. It's just like trout fishing."

"But the jack might lose to the queen, sir. Admittedly, you have relinquished the lead to the 'safe' hand, and he cannot attack the hearts to advantage."

"Exactly, Jeeves."

"But suppose, sir, that his queen was bare?"

"I say, Jeeves. That's dashed racy."

"A singleton, sir. That would mean East has four and when he gains the lead, he will play a heart through your queen, with rather unfortunate results."

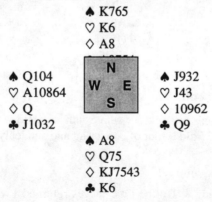

	♠ K765	
	♡ K6	
	◇ A8	

♠ Q104		♠ J932
♡ A10864		♡ J43
◇ Q		◇ 10962
♣ J1032		♣ Q9

	♠ A8	
	♡ Q75	
	◇ KJ7543	
	♣ K6	

"Jeeves, this isn't fair. Everytime a fellow plays something, you cook up some awful distribution and make him look an ass."

"I'm afraid bridge is like that, sir."

"Yes. What was it that Scots laddie said? The mice thing."

"'The best laid schemes o' mice and men gang aft aglay', sir. However, Burns, being in the whisky trade, was not familiar with safety plays."

"Jeeves, you've lost me."

"To allow for the possibility of a bare queen with West, sir, you should cross to your hand at trick two, and play a low diamond towards dummy. Now, if West drops the queen, you duck, sir."

"Duck, Jeeves?"

"The mechanism is explained on page thirty-two of the book you read earlier, sir."

"But are you actually suggesting I let the blighter make his bare queen?"

"One must speculate to accumulate, sir. If he now attacks hearts you will come to ten tricks."

I downed the whisky and soda which Jeeves had thoughtfully provided.

"Jeeves, was that hand very advanced?"

"It is a matter of relativity, sir. If we were to call it advanced, how should we describe a smother play?"

"With great difficulty. But surely the Hon. Lat. can't know all that stuff?"

"At Roedean they talked of little else. She was the star pupil of her year, sir."

"Jeeves, why didn't you tell me this before?"

"I have just telephoned the Diogenes Club, sir. They told me that your fiancée has already been noticed by Lady Rhodes."

My head was spinning. To be told you had to let a chap win tricks with bare queens was bad enough. But to learn that you had a fiancée who took to such notions like a duck to water was a body blow. There was only one remedy.

"Another W and S please, Jeeves."

"Certainly, sir."

"Jeeves, she must eat an awful lot of fish."

"Lady Rhodes, sir?"

"The Hon. Lat."

"I believe she is partial to *saumon en croute*, sir."

"How can such a large brain fit into a sweet little head like that?"

"An anatomical curiosity, sir."

"Just as I was about to put it. A pity, Jeeves. I admit she's no Garbo."

"A trifle too short, sir."

"Not even a Claudette Colbert."

"Her cheekbones are not as pronounced, sir. And if I might say so . . . ."

"Say away, Jeeves."

"She is reputed to be merciless to her partners. None of them has yet committed suicide, sir, but informed opinion suggests that it is only a matter of time."

"Good Lord!"

"Sir?"

I rose. Courageous action was called for, and in such circs we Woosters do not shrink.

"Jeeves," I said. "That three months' cruise you've been suggesting we take. When does the boat sail?"

"Tomorrow morning, sir. I take it that we are contemplating a safety play?"

"You may reserve two places immediately."

"I have already done so, sir."

13

BRIDGE IN THE FIFTH DIMENSION

"No one is deeply stirred by the fate of lifeless puppets around a paper diagram," wrote Victor Mollo. "How much more exciting to watch a duel between man and man, following the Hideous Hog as he strives to squeeze or smother his arch enemy, Papa the Greek."

Bridge in the Menagerie was not the first work to be written on this premise, but it reached new heights of outrageous characterisation. The Hog's detractors describe him as arrogant, bombastic, gluttonous and selfish. Then they start on his defects.

Why is it then that we cannot help liking him? Perhaps it is because of his modesty. In an uncharacteristic moment, he once admitted that the entire Italian Blue Team were his equals. This revealed yet another of his short-comings, his inaccuracy. Garozzo and Belladonna have been known to err, and nobody would dare to accuse HH of doing that.

He classified some of his plays as fourth dimensional in defence or dummy play. But why not a fifth? This would involve inspiring a worthy dupe, such as Themistocles Papadopoulos, to conceive a fourth dimensional coup, only to be thwarted by a fifth dimensional counter.

The Hog Takes The Fifth

I gazed longingly at my glass of Chateau Margaux '61 as it vanished into the Hog's capacious gullet. We were at Gorgons, guests of their Junior Kibitzer, Aubrey the Aardvark, renowned for his passion for oriental chocolate-covered ants.

Having dined soberly on foie gras with truffles, lobster thermidor, a brace of Aylesbury ducks and a Chateaubriand for two, HH was in benign mood as he selected his main course.

"That odious Greek!" he snarled. "Do you know what he accused me of?"

"Raising the Rueful Rabbit in no trumps?" suggested Colin the Corgi, whose gift for sarcasm was rapidly establishing his reputation as an expert.

The Hog snorted. "Papa," he said, "has the temerity to suggest I gloat over my brilliancies. I! Who can no more help performing them than Dickens could help writing Moby Dick"

He poured a millimetre of Aloxe Corton into his empty glass and deftly exchanged it for Colin's full one. "And if," he added, "I should modestly draw attention to the occasional magnum opus, what of it? How else could lesser ... I mean my fellow players, appreciate its finer points? Let me show you an example."

Seizing the Rabbit's signed photograph of Rhoda Lederer he scribbled two hands:

♠ AJ65
♡ –
◊ K10953
♣ AK76

♠ K104
♡ AKQ108753
◊ –
♣ 42

"You are South, declarer in 7♡. The main feature of an otherwise dull auction is that East doubled North's diamonds, presumably for a lead. West obediently leads the ◊J and you cover with the ◊K. East surprisingly plays low. How do you proceed?"

He chewed contentedly on one of Aubrey's devilled kidneys. "The crocodile coup," murmured the Corgi. "Swallowing his partner's entrée."

The Rabbit, unhampered by any conscious thought process, was the first to speak. "I ruff," he said. "Not for any reason, you understand, but because East didn't cover, so he doesn't want me to, so I do."

"You could be right, RR," agreed the Aardvark, who had been showing such promise in recent post-mortems that the Senior Kibitzer's chair seemed well within his grasp. "East played low because he expects a trick from another source. He must hold something like ♡J964, in which case declarer must reduce his own trumps. After ruffing and laying down the ♡AK he sees he needs four entries to dummy, the ♣AK and the ♠AJ. Obviously he must play the ♠K first, then grit his teeth and finesse the ♠J. But for HH that is a routine masterpiece. After trick eleven, with the lead in dummy, his ♡Q10 are poised over East's ♡J9. However ..."

To leave Aubrey free to continue his discourse, the Hog considerately relieved him of his last kidney.

" ... However," the Aardvark continued, "there is considerable risk that East has a doubleton spade and will ruff the third round."

There was a profound silence, or there would have been had the Hog not been enjoying Aubrey's kidneys so much. Aubrey thought feverishly. The honour of the Gorgons, and his own career could be at stake.

"I have it!" he cried. "All we need to do is discard a spade at trick one and ruff a diamond at trick two."

"Which spade?" asked the Corgi with a quizzical smile.

"The king," responded the Aardvark promptly. "Otherwise when declarer leads towards the ♠AJ an adroit West will put up the ♠Q and kill a vital entry."

"A superb analysis," said the Hog. "Matched by declarer, who was the textbook technician, Themistocles Papadopoulos."

"I thought this was an example of one of your own triumphs," Colin objected.

"It was," the Hog sneered as he added the East and West hands. "I happened to be East."

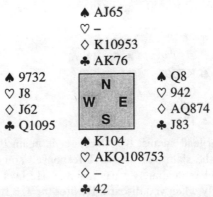

```
                    ♠ AJ65
                    ♡ -
                    ◇ K10953
                    ♣ AK76
    ♠ 9732                          ♠ Q8
    ♡ J8          N                 ♡ 942
    ◇ J62       W   E               ◇ AQ874
    ♣ Q1095        S                ♣ J83
                    ♠ K104
                    ♡ AKQ108753
                    ◇ -
                    ♣ 42
```

"I knew Papa was void in diamonds because he had cue-bid clubs, a routine deception in which he has shown touching faith over the years. So I had to take my ♠Q to defeat the slam. By allowing the ◇K to hold I tempted him to take the spade finesse and step briefly into the fourth dimension. I of course was playing in the fifth."

"But you can't blame Papa," said the Rabbit. "Because you're always fooling all of us. I mean, er, even I ..."

"Are you defending that charlatan?" thundered the Hog. "After he played so atrociously? His ♠K at trick one was a *felo de se*. You haven't asked me who was West."

"Who was West?" grinned the Corgi.

"Walter the Walrus, the worst player in the Western Hemisphere. Can you imagine him rising with a queen in second position? He would regard it as an immoral act, like failing to use defensive signals to assist declarer. Therefore Papa should have discarded a small spade, like any genuine master ... " He bowed modestly. "... Then he would have had all thirteen top tricks. And in that situation, even RR, playing at the top of his form ...."

He left the gracious compliment unfinished, but the Rueful Rabbit turned crimson with pleasure. The Hog turned to Aubrey.

"I absolve you of all blame," he announced graciously. "Your solution was based on the assumption that West was a better player than yourself, and it is extremely unfortunate that on this occasion you were wrong. To show you I bear no malice, I will accept another glass of this exquisite burgundy. While you are pouring it and we wait for another bottle, here is another hand with a similar theme:

```
              ♠ A532
              ♡ 7
              ◇ A105
              ♣ 98643
♠.KQJ98
♡ 6
◇ Q872
♣ J72
```

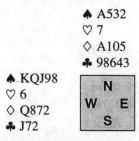

You are West, on lead against 6♡. Declarer is again Papa, who opened 2♣ and leapt to the slam over the 2NT response. You lead the ♠K. He plays the ♠A and immediately ruffs a spade. He lays down the ♡AK, nodding knowingly when you discard. He fires the ◇3 from hand. Over to you."

"I play the ◊Q," said the Rabbit. "If the answer was a small diamond, well I mean, you wouldn't give it to us as a problem, would you? At least I..."

"You have a genius for compressing the smallest amount of thought into the largest number of words," beamed the Hog, and RR blushed happily at his second accolade.

"And this time he could be right," said the Corgi. "It looks as if declarer has something like ♠8 ♡AKQ10863 ◊KJ6 ♣A5. He needs two diamond entries for his trump coup and RR's ◊Q has accidentally put paid to one of them."

The Hog was by now purring. "But Papa did not hold the hand you envisaged," he informed us, and within seconds, on the linen tablecloth, the full deal was revealed:

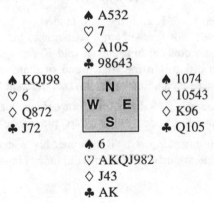

```
                    ♠ A532
                    ♡ 7
                    ◊ A105
                    ♣ 98643
      ♠ KQJ98          N           ♠ 1074
      ♡ 6                           ♡ 10543
      ◊ Q872        W     E        ◊ K96
      ♣ J72            S            ♣ Q105
                    ♠ 6
                    ♡ AKQJ982
                    ◊ J43
                    ♣ AK
```

"You see it now, don't you? Barring a very favourable lie in the diamond suit the contract is doomed unless West can be persuaded to play the queen. All Papa needed was a West with a singleton heart and enough *savoir faire* to be bamboozled."

"Surely not you?" scoffed the Corgi.

"West," said the Hog, "was Karapet, the Free Armenian." He paused, not for effect, but to wash down a mouthful of crepes with a glassful of the Rabbit's Chateau d'Yquem. "He was just clever enough to swallow the bait. Yet he didn't. Why not? Because once again I was East, the player you have all overlooked."

As we wondered what East had to do with it, the Hog looked around the table, as if searching for signs of intelligent life. Finding none, he continued:

(The hand is repeated for convenience.)

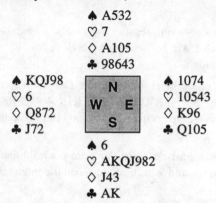

```
            ♠ A532
            ♡ 7
            ◇ A105
            ♣ 98643
♠ KQJ98                    ♠ 1074
♡ 6          N            ♡ 10543
◇ Q872    W     E         ◇ K96
♣ J72        S            ♣ Q105
            ♠ 6
            ♡ AKQJ982
            ◇ J43
            ♣ AK
```

"When Papa played his ♡K and my ♡10 landed on Karapet's spade discard ..." He paused, not for Aubrey's Armagnac, but for effect. "That Greek could scarcely conceal his rage. It told Karapet that there was no trump coup in the offing. On the first round of diamonds he played an innocuous deuce and we came inevitably to two tricks in the suit."

"HH," said the Aardvark, "I salute you. Your defence was Wellingtonian. But you must admit on this occasion that Papa played well."

"True," said the Hog, generously. "But he met his Waterloo, did he not? Still," he laughed uproariously, " he always did fancy himself as Napoleon."

14
STAR TREK

Captain's log: Stardate 2335

The Enterprise has contacted the remote planet Alcon.

Our mission: to boldly persuade their government to join the Galactic Federation.

The humanoid Alcons have a game-playing culture, promotion to high office depending on success in a wide range of intellectual contests. Bridge, which they learned from an intrepid terrestrial explorer, is the one pastime which they share with Earth. They have boldly challenged us to a match and their acceptance of Federation membership could depend on the outcome.

The Enterprise has some keen players, including one galactic and two inter-planetary masters. They are all in practice, as we have had no red alerts for eight episodes.

However...

The Mediocrity of Captain Kirk

"Bones," said Kirk. "I'd like you to play in the match against the Alcons. Your partner will be Mr. Spock."

"Jim, you can't be serious!" McCoy exploded. "How can you expect me to sit opposite that insufferable Vulcan calculating machine? Have you seen the way he raises that quizzical eyebrow every time I play against the odds?"

A beautifully-timed boyish smile appeared on Kirk's handsome face. He enjoyed the conflict between his unemotional first officer and the whimsical ship's doctor. "It will be an eccentric pairing," he agreed. "I'm hoping the Alcons will find it as tricky to handle as I do."

The imperturbable Spock entered, carrying a sheaf of papers. "Gentleman," he announced. "I have completed my analysis of the Alcons' bidding methods and my recommendations for the team selection. Ensigns Kirillov and Muller ..."

"Our opponents equate rank with game-playing ability," Kirk objected. "They will be offended if they are asked to play against junior officers."

"Nevertheless, Captain, the two ensigns have developed an interesting version of the Klinger multicoloured bids."

"Surely you mean Klingon?"

"No, sir. Klinger was a noted player during the early days of contract. He came from a remote part of your planet known as Australia, famous for its unusual fauna and an alcoholic beverage called lager."

"Anyway," said Kirk impatiently, "our team will be Scotty, myself and you, partnered by Doctor McCoy."

Spock raised a quizzical eyebrow. "Fascinating. A combination of pure logic and the somewhat bizarre methods which the good doctor likes to describe as flair."

"Why you inhuman, pointy-eared, desiccated mass of unemotional circuitry!"

"There's no time for compliments, Bones" said Kirk. "I'm due to meet Scotty for a system discussion. I suggest you do the same."

"Not necessary," replied Spock. "I can provide the Doctor with an instantaneous knowledge of my system through my Vulcan mind-meld."

"Negative!" snapped McCoy. "You bid what you've got, and I'll provide the flair. And watch those confounded eyebrows. The only thing I want to see raised are my opening bids."

One star-week later, the Enterprise team beamed boldly down to find that their scrupulous Alcon hosts had chosen four players of exactly equivalent rank to the ship's quartet.

Spock and McCoy were soon faced with a fascinating defensive problem:

```
                    ♠ AK5
                    ♡ J2
                    ◇ 643
                    ♣ AJ962
    ♠ 8764          ┌─────────┐      ♠ J
    ♡ AQ953         │    N    │      ♡ 1086
    ◇ 98            │ W     E │      ◇ AKQJ52
    ♣ 85            │    S    │      ♣ 743
                    └─────────┘
                    ♠ Q10932
                    ♡ K74
                    ◇ 107
                    ♣ KQ10
```

Game All. Dealer West.

West	North	East	South
McCoy		*Spock*	
Pass	1♣	2◇	2♠
Pass	3♠	Pass	Pass
Dble	All Pass		

Contract 3♠. ◇9 led.

The Enterprise pair were playing strong jump overcalls and Spock's 2◇ was a calculated overbid. He won the first trick with the ◇J, swiftly computed every possible distribution and followed with the ◇A and K.

South, an inveterate pessimist, considered ruffing with the ♠9, until it occurred to him that he might lose control of the hand. He visualised the following East/West holdings:

```
    ♠ J876          ┌─────────┐      ♠ 4
    ♡ Q10953        │    N    │      ♡ A86
    ◇ 98            │ W     E │      ◇ AKQJ52
    ♣ 85            │    S    │      ♣ 743
                    └─────────┘
```

West would decline to over-ruff and discard a club. It would now be fatal to draw trumps, and playing on clubs would be no better. McCoy would ruff the second round and put Spock in with the ♡A to obtain another ruff. So the Alcon decided on a cunning safety play, and trumped with the ♠2. When McCoy confirmed his suspicions by discarding the ♣5, he ran the ♠10 with complete confidence, which was rudely shattered when Spock won with the ♠J and switched to a heart through declarer's king for one down and plus 200.

"An excellent defence, Doctor," said Spock. "Obviously you deduced South's holding from his vulnerable bidding and concluded that I must hold the ♠J to defeat the contract. Your subsequent deceptive play was the result of impeccable deductive logic, worthy of a Vulcan."

"Logic be damned!" growled McCoy. "When declarer played the ♠2, I guessed he wanted me to over-ruff, so I didn't. It was impeccable, plain orneriness, worthy of a Texan."

Spock made no comment, and his eyebrow control was exemplary.

In the other room, Kirk made 3♠ with an overtrick, by the less expert play of ruffing with the ♠9 and drawing trumps.

The scores were tied as the last board was played.

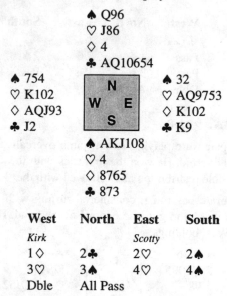

```
                        ♠ Q96
                        ♡ J86
                        ◇ 4
                        ♣ AQ10654
        ♠ 754          ┌─────────┐        ♠ 32
        ♡ K102         │    N    │        ♡ AQ9753
        ◇ AQJ93        │ W     E │        ◇ K102
        ♣ J2           │    S    │        ♣ K9
                        └─────────┘
                        ♠ AKJ108
                        ♡ 4
                        ◇ 8765
                        ♣ 873
```

West	North	East	South
Kirk		Scotty	
1◇	2♣	2♡	2♠
3♡	3♠	4♡	4♠
Dble	All Pass		

Contract 4♠. ♡2 led.

Kirk, sitting West, doubled in order to boldly demonstrate his leadership. He led the ♡2. Winning with the ♡A, Scotty returned the ♡5. Declarer ruffed and immediately led a club to dummy's ♣10. Scotty, his honest Highland face radiating innocence, smoothly played the ♣9, baring the king. Now the Alcon, seeing every prospect of an overtrick which might well clinch the match, drew trumps and led a second club, covering West's ♣J with the queen. The Chief Engineer triumphantly won with the ♣K, and four rounds of diamonds defeated the contract by three tricks.

"Commander," remarked the sporting Alcon declarer in the fluent English mysteriously spoken by every alien race discovered by the Enterprise, "I'm lost in admiration."

"Oh, it was nae so difficult," Scott modestly replied. "Ye were marked with a singleton heart and five winning spades, so I threw a wee spanner in the works – it's an old engineer's trick. Nae need ta blame yoursel' laddie. Och aye the noo."

Whether Scotty was right to absolve declarer was about to be revealed in the other room, where Spock played in the same contract, also on the lead of a small heart.

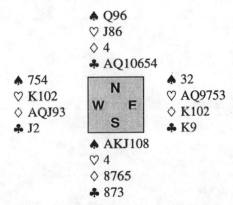

                    ♠ Q96
                    ♡ J86
                    ◇ 4
                    ♣ AQ10654
    ♠ 754   ♠ 32
    ♡ K102   ♡ AQ9753
    ◇ AQJ93   ◇ K102
    ♣ J2   ♣ K9
                    ♠ AKJ108
                    ♡ 4
                    ◇ 8765
                    ♣ 873

Ruffing the second round, Spock also led a small club to the ♣10 at trick three, and the Alcon sitting East also followed smoothly with the ♣9. But the Vulcan, instead of drawing trumps, instantly led dummy's ◇4. Now the defence was helpless. Whatever they played, Spock would win, return to his hand if necessary and repeat the club finesse. When it lost, dummy's spades would be on hand to take care of a diamond switch. It would be a simple matter now to draw trumps and enjoy the winning clubs on the table.

McCoy's congratulations were gruff. "Now don't tell me that wasn't an example of flair," he said.

"I'm sorry to disappoint you, Doctor, but it was elementary Vulcan logic. I reasoned that to an expert of the calibre of the officer on my right, so soon to be a worthy member of the Federation, to bare the ♣K would be routine brilliancy. Therefore at trick four, the ◇4 was the only rational play."

Later when the Enterprise received the plaudits of the Alcon players and officials, Kirk was taken aside by their non-playing captain.

"Captain Kirk," he said. "Without wishing to offend you, I noticed that all three of your team-mates made several excellent plays, while you did nothing of remotely expert quality. How come you are the ship's captain?"

Kirk favoured him with that famous sophomore grin. "A good question, sir," he replied. "I believe in the next episode I will demote myself to yeoman."

15
THE AGONY COLUMN

This famous and deadly hand from the 1930s highlights the need for an 'agony aunt' to advise married couples who have made the bridge table their personal battleground.

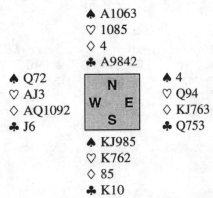

                ♠ A1063
                ♡ 1085
                ◇ 4
                ♣ A9842

♠ Q72   ♠ 4
♡ AJ3   ♡ Q94
◇ AQ1092   ◇ KJ763
♣ J6   ♣ Q753

                ♠ KJ985
                ♡ K762
                ◇ 85
                ♣ K10

The contract was 4♠ by South. West led the ◇A and switched to the ♣J.

Mr. John G. Bennett of Kansas City took in hand, led the ♠J and, when this was not covered rose with dummy's ♠A. After he had gone two down, he quarrelled with his wife, who shot him dead. The contract is easy to make double dummy, but there are different views on how it should have been played.

The following letters illustrate the saying, 'Never criticise your husband's imperfections. They were the qualities which prevented him from getting a better wife.'

Dear Aunt Marjorie,

My husband snores, drinks like a fish, chases anything in a skirt and,, whenever I express my disapproval, he hits me back.

But what really bugs me is his bidding. He is (there's no other word for it) a contract hog.

This hand is typical of him.

Game All. Dealer East

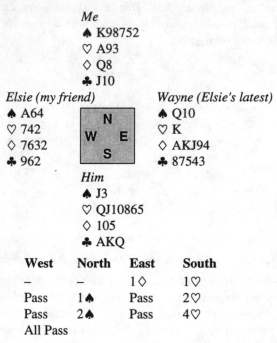

Me
♠ K98752
♡ A93
◇ Q8
♣ J10

Elsie (my friend)
♠ A64
♡ 742
◇ 7632
♣ 962

Wayne (Elsie's latest)
♠ Q10
♡ K
◇ AKJ94
♣ 87543

Him
♠ J3
♡ QJ10865
◇ 105
♣ AKQ

West	North	East	South
–	–	1◇	1♡
Pass	1♠	Pass	2♡
Pass	2♠	Pass	4♡
All Pass			

I know I should have gone four spades, but I didn't fancy watching him squirm in 5♡ doubled, not at 5p a hundred.

He played the hand like a complete prat. Elsie led the ◇6 and followed with the ◇7 on the second round. Bert (my husband), said afterwards that this showed she had four diamonds on their methods, but I can't see what difference that made. Anyway, he scratched his head (another of his annoying habits – and he's got dandruff) played the ♡Q and when this wasn't covered he put up the ♡A, dropping Wayne's bare king!

I know he didn't peek because we had a slight argument that evening and his glasses got broken. Where was I? Oh yes. He drew trumps and led a spade from hand. When Elsie played low he won with the ♠K, gave me one of his smug looks and claimed ten tricks.When I asked him why he played like a merchant banker he said only an expert would understand.

You've probably read between the lines and guessed our marriage isn't all it should be. My question is, Marjorie – have I got grounds for a divorce?

Downtrodden of Walthamstow

Dear Downtrodden,

I don't think you could obtain a divorce on bridge grounds. The judge might carp at your rebidding your spades twice. If he's really biased he might even think that ♡A93 is good support for your husband's vulnerable overcall. I'm not saying I'd agree with him, but it is a view.

Bert's bidding is not above reproach, but a clever lawyer might advise him to testify that because his glasses had been smashed as a result of your mild rebuke, he had mis-sorted his hand.

As for the play, Downtrodden. I am afraid I have some bad news for you.

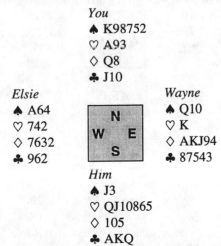

You
♠ K98752
♡ A93
◇ Q8
♣ J10

Elsie
♠ A64
♡ 742
◇ 7632
♣ 962

Wayne
♠ Q10
♡ K
◇ AKJ94
♣ 87543

Him
♠ J3
♡ QJ10865
◇ 105
♣ AKQ

Bert almost certainly reasoned that the contract could not be made unless Elsie held the ♠A. Think about it. And if she did have this card, then Wayne (he sounds dishy!) with only five diamonds, needed the ♡K to justify his opening bid. So declarer's only chance was to play him for a singleton.

This is an example of what divorce lawyers call 'card play by assumption'.

It is not the most advanced instance I have seen, but it was rather neat, so you'll have to try to nail Bert on adultery.

But my question is – are you sure he hasn't got a defence to that?

Yours

Marjorie

Dear Aunt Marjorie

Thanks for your letter. It came as a disappointment to me, but I see what you mean about Card Play by Consumption – it sounds typical of Bert. But after what happened yesterday, I think I've got him for mental cruelty.

North/South Game. Dealer South.

Him

♠ 3
♡ 10754
◇ K642
♣ AQ107

Darren (Wayne's replacement) *Elsie (my friend)*

♠ Q1082		♠ J9765
♡ KJ963	**N**	♡ Q2
◇ Q87	**W E**	◇ 105
♣ K	**S**	♣ 9865

Me

♠ AK4
♡ A8
◇ AJ93
♣ J432

West	North	East	South
–	–	–	1NT
2♡	Dble	Pass	2NT
Pass	3NT	Pass	Pass
Dble	Pass	Pass	Rdble
All Pass			

Notice his selfish double of 2♡, when he should have been raising my no trumps. Anyway, Darren led the ♡6 and I ducked Elsie's ♡Q. (You can tell I've played before, can't you?) I won the heart continuation and led the ♣J, covering the ♣K with dummy's ♣A. Finding East with four clubs was my first bit of rotten luck. I now played the ◇K and finessed the ◇J. Of course, Darren had to have the ◇Q, didn't he? And when he cashed his winning hearts, I was one down.

Now I think you'll agree, when it comes to ducking and finessing, I know my stuff. But Bert said the contact was cold for two overtricks!

Surely this constitutes grounds for divorce?

Dear Downtrodden

Assuming that at trick one you selected the ♡4 from dummy, your play up to this point was perfect. It was only when you ducked from hand that you fell from the high standard you had set. The play of the ♡A is automatic in this situation and in any case the Rule of Eleven might have told you that the ♡10 was a second stopper. I recommend that you look up 'Rule of Eleven', and, to be on the safe side, 'stopper'.

Your next fall from grace did not occur until trick three. You really should have led a low club from hand, to cater for a singleton ♣K with West.

Now we come to your third tiny departure from competence. A better plan would have been to cross to your ♠A and to lead the ◊J from hand. This is known as an 'avoidance play', preventing the danger hand from gaining the lead. As the cards lay, this would have earned you an overtrick.

I hesitate to recommend a more expert line which would have enabled you to recover from your early wrong views. Cash the ♣Q10, forcing two discards from West. Now play-off the ♠AK and when West follows both times you have a complete count of the hand, and you can see that he is strip-squeezed. You exit with a heart, and have the satisfaction of making your contract by forcing him to lead away from his ◊Q.

Now for the question of mental cruelty. Legal precedents suggest that when a player is responsible for an adverse swing of this magnitude (minus 400 could have been plus 2,000), his or her spouse is entitled to give voice to criticism rather more scathing than 'the contract was cold for two overtricks'.

In the classic case of Jones versus Jones (1954) the judge ruled that the expression, 'You played like a mentally retarded sponge', used to deprecate dummy play of a similar standard to your own, was not only justified but an insult to mentally retarded sponges.

Have you considered giving up bridge in favour of Trivial Pursuit?

Yours, for the very last time, I hope,

Marjorie

16
THE JAZZ AGE

F. Scott Fitzgerald was the leading recorder of the Jazz Age. Discovering that he was part of a generation which believed that all gods were dead and that all wars had been fought, his remedy was to write a best seller and splash the royalties on a glorious spending spree with his wife, Zelda.

This provided the inspiration for two great novels, The Great Gatsby *and* Tender is the Night, *both about attractive, successful men (like Scott) ruined by destructively beautiful women (like Zelda) who smashed up things and people and then retreated into their money.*

As Fitzgerald's talent slowly disappeared into the bottom of an endless champagne cocktail, he maintained that his marriage was a great success – 'ecstatic and miserable'. When Zelda wrote insultingly of Scott, she often began, 'Mr Fitzgerald – I understand that is how he spells his name ....'

The Fitzgeralds' lifestyle did not endear them to everyone, and particularly not to the man who wrote:

> *If F. Scott and Zelda were class,*
> *Cellini made things out of brass,*
> *And Dacron is fur,*
> *Airwick smells like myrrh,*
> *And plastic's as good as stained glass.*

Bridge with the Divers

Rosemary walked along the pleasant Riviera shore, back to the rose-coloured, orchid-shaped hotel, with its deferential palms, which she loved when she and her mother took afternoon tea in the achromatic sunshine. As she came to the pink and cream terrace, she saw three expensively simple people sitting at a table covered in sea green baize.

"We know who you are," said the brown-haired woman. "You're Rosemary, the girl who makes all those marvellous moving pictures."

Rosemary watched her idly shuffling a pack of cards, but her gaze was soon drawn from the delicate, ivory hands to the Rodinesque face, sculpted into a beauty so complete that a single slip would have been an affront to its chiselled perfection. Rosemary instantly loathed the bitch.

"Good morning," said the fine, hard man in the tight swimming costume. "You have been named – and addressed – by my wife, Nicole. I'm Dick Diver, and we are desperately seeking a fourth for bridge."

His blue eyes regarded her from his reddish, weather-burned face with an interest so intense that, wooed by the elusive Irish melody in his voice, Rosemary chose him, and, seeing this, Nicole gave a feline purr of antipathy to warn rival predators that he was already possessed.

"You mustn't get too fond of Dick," she said.

"So my mother told me," Rosemary replied, as she became aware of the third person at the table, a man, elegant, shadowy and strangely withdrawn.

Dick, watching her eyes said, "This is Jay Gatsby."

Rosemary gave a puzzled frown, and said, "But surely he's from ..."

"A different book?" Dick gave a musical, thousand dollar laugh. "Yes, I suppose he is. Perhaps he'll tell you how he got here after a rubber or two. Shall we cut for partners?"

Nicole drew a lowly deuce and Rosemary gave a lovely little shiver of her face as she drew the king of spades and placed it in daring proximity to Dick's queen. But Gatsby drew an ace and won the dubious privilege of partnering Rosemary.

As he dealt, she could sense the deep sadness of a man branded bootlegger, gangster and nouveau riche by a rigid East Coast society, the ultimate evolution of a class whose family trees went all the way back to the previous generation.

Rosemary picked up her cards with nervous pink fingers as she tried frantically to recall all the wise things her mother had taught her.

"Always cover an honour with an honour. Lead your partner's suit, even if you have a void. Change your underwear every day. Never open without three and a half honour tricks. And always get the young man's name and address." The resonant adumbrations of her mother's experience imposed themselves on Rosemary's fragile naïveté.

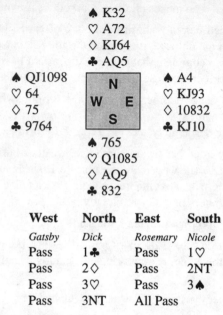

```
                    ♠ K32
                    ♡ A72
                    ◇ KJ64
                    ♣ AQ5
  ♠ QJ1098                          ♠ A4
  ♡ 64            N                 ♡ KJ93
  ◇ 75        W       E             ◇ 10832
  ♣ 9764          S                 ♣ KJ10
                    ♠ 765
                    ♡ Q1085
                    ◇ AQ9
                    ♣ 832
```

West	North	East	South
Gatsby	*Dick*	*Rosemary*	*Nicole*
Pass	1♣	Pass	1♡
Pass	2◇	Pass	2NT
Pass	3♡	Pass	3♠
Pass	3NT	All Pass	

The Great Gatsby assessed his three points with the cool, impassive demeanour of a man who knew the man who fixed the World Series. He said neither 'pass' or 'no bid', but simply shook his head, as if being in the wrong book had deprived him of the right to speak.

Dick Diver, not ashamed to emulate his social inferiors, opened a Vanderbilt Club and, after Nicole's heart response, reversed with a careless gaiety which was part of his secret bargain with the Gods. Nicole's two no trumps was a product of her stygian psychosis, as revealed in Book Two, and her bid of three spades showed that it was incurable.

Against three no trumps, Gatsby led the ♠Q, ominously black. Nicole called for dummy's deuce. Rosemary knew that she was the world's worst player; her mother had told her so. But she also knew that the queen was an honour and had to be covered with an honour, so she played her ace and dutifully returned the four.

Nicole, winning with dummy's ♠K, led the ♡A. Rosemary, faithful to the maternal dictum, covered this with her ♡K and Nicole, in a flash of deductive brilliance, recognised it as a coup designed to create an entry to Gatsby's putative ♡J and his long fatal spades. Abandoning hearts, therefore, she crossed to hand with a diamond and led a small club to the queen. Rosemary's ecstasy was beyond belief. She covered this card with her king, and returned the ♣J, continuing with the ♣10 when the trick was ducked.

Nicole cashed her winning diamonds, noticing that Gatsby discarded two precious spades. She was sure that he had kept one spade winner and the ♡J, jealously guarded, and she felt the sensuous inner warmth which is the gift of those who have their man exactly where they want him. Flushed, her lips parted in anticipation. Nicole led a spade to Gatsby's queen and was about to spread her hand when, enigmatically, he produced a club to set the contract by a single trick.

"A superb deception," Dick said, smiling at Rosemary, and it was Rosemary's turn with the sensuous inner warmth. There were no bouquets for Gatsby's thoughtful defence, but he bore the neglect with practised stoicism. Ten years of waiting for Daisy Buchanan had taught him to expect nothing from the world's bazaar.

"Do you mind if we stop now?" asked Rosemary breathlessly.

"Is the excitement too much for you?" asked Nicole, her voice low, almost harsh.

"I have to meet my mother."

"Then you must come back tomorrow for another hand. By the end of the season we might finish a whole rubber," said Nicole, her voice harsh, almost low.

In her mother's lap afterwards, Rosemary cried and cried.

"Mother, I'm desperately in love with him. And he's married and his wife bid three no trumps, but I beat it by an awful fluke – and it's all just hopeless."

"Did you remember to cover an honour with an honour, dear?"

"Yes mother. Three times."

"And your underwear?"

"Clean this morning, mother."

"And did you lead back your partner's suit?"

"Yes, mother. It was spades."

"Good. And did you get the young man's name and address?"

"Yes, mother. He lives in the South of France."

"Then I'm sure everything will turn out fine."

17
WIND IN THE WILLOWS

Kenneth Grahame was a remarkable Scot, who became Secretary of the Bank of England before he was forty, an obvious qualification for writing one of the best-loved books for children in English. His anthropomorphic animals make ideal bridge characters. The Badger would be pragmatic and direct, a sort of underground S.J. Simon. Ratty would be an enthusiastic scientist, bursting to communicate the latest conventions. Mole would be a modest underbidder. Toad would be the kind of player whose sheer blind luck cancelled out his inept play, in anticipation of the Rueful Rabbit.

And of course the wild-wooders would make the perfect villains.

Bridge at Toad Hall

"Here's-a-scorecard-for-the-Rat, here's-a-scorecard-for-the-mole, here's-a-scorecard-for-the-Badger, here's-a-scorecard-for-the-Toad,. Here's-a-pencil-for ..."

"All right, Ratty," said the Badger. "You can stop fussing. We're only playing the Stoats and Weasels."

"But Badger," said the Mole, "I know you're always right, but they have won the Wild Woods teams twice running."

"Yes, but this is the first time we've entered. And what are we going to do to them tonight?'

"We're going to learn 'em!" cried the Toad.

"*Teach* them," said the Rat. "And I've already composed a victory song. It's called 'Ducks-are-a-doubling'. Shall I sing it?"

'Not now," said the Badger peevishly. "As Captain ..."

"Can't I be Captain?" whined the Toad.

"As Captain," continued the Badger, "I want to hold a team talk. You first, Mole. Now I want none of your underbids. If you've got 'em, bid 'em!"

"I'll try, Badger."

"I know you will. You're a good, sensible animal. And when you lead against a slam, attack!"

The Rat looked shocked. "Surely not against a grand slam?"

The Badger silenced him with a look. "And as for you, Rat, if I open a club and you've got seven hearts to the ace-king, bid four hearts. Never mind your fancy approaches. I've never liked 'em and I never will. Bid what you can make."

"Is it the same as 'if you've got 'em bid 'em' Badger?"

"No it isn't. It means good old fashioned blitzing."

The Toad was feeling left out. "Haven't you any advice for me, Badger?" he asked, hopefully.

Badger regarded him kindly. "No Toad, I haven't, because I don't want to ruin your confidence," he said. "Besides, the first mistake you make and I'm replacing you with the Otter."

At that moment the Otter entered, carrying duplicate boards. "Here you are, my fine fellows. Twenty-four boards. And remember, Badger, you said I could take Toad's place from board two onwards."

Toad flung himself on the sofa and sobbed into the cushions.

"Cheer up. Toad, " the Badger comforted him. "If we're more than forty IMPs up, I'll put you in again for board twenty-four, provided you stop saying 'poop, poop' every time you take a finesse."

The Toad cheered up, and was about to burst into song when the Stoats and the Weasels arrived. They looked crafty and mean, and were armed to the teeth with bridge books, rule books, convention cards and eyeshades. They wore matching blazers with 'WWTC' embroidered on the breast pockets. The Toad went green with envy.

The first board was a triumph for the Badger.

Love All. Dealer North.

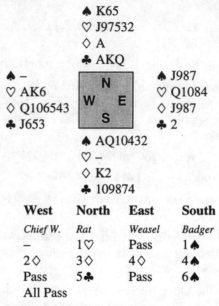

                    ♠ K65
                    ♡ J97532
                    ◇ A
                    ♣ AKQ
    ♠ –   ♠ J987
    ♡ AK6   ♡ Q1084
    ◇ Q106543   ◇ J987
    ♣ J653   ♣ 2
                    ♠ AQ10432
                    ♡ –
                    ◇ K2
                    ♣ 109874

West	North	East	South
Chief W.	*Rat*	*Weasel*	*Badger*
–	1♡	Pass	1♠
2◇	3◇	4◇	4♠
Pass	5♣	Pass	6♠
All Pass			

Contract 6♠ by South. Lead ♡A.

The Badger frowned at the Rat's bidding, but cheered up when he saw dummy. He ruffed the ♡A and laid down the ♠A, pausing when West discarded the ◇3. He could draw trumps, picking up East's ♠J, and play off his minor suit winners. But if the clubs broke badly – quite likely on the bidding – he would have to use his last trump to regain the lead and would lose two more tricks to the ♣J and the ♡K.

So at trick three Badger crossed to the ♠K and played off the ◇A and the ♣A. He drew trumps and cashed his last spade, throwing the ♣KQ from dummy. He led a club, losing to West's jack, but he still had a trump to regain the lead and make the last three tricks with his established clubs.

"Well played!" cried Rat. "Capital!"

"A routine unblock," snapped the Chief Weasel.

The play was not routine for the Stoat in room two, who went one down in the same contract, but the Toad was dropped for poop-pooping when he took the setting trick with the ♡K.

However, the Toad Hall team forged so far ahead that the good-hearted Badger let the Toad take his place for the final board.

Game All. Dealer South.

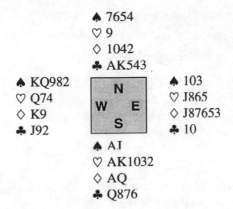

```
                      ♠ 7654
                      ♡ 9
                      ◇ 1042
                      ♣ AK543
   ♠ KQ982                          ♠ 103
   ♡ Q74          N                 ♡ J865
   ◇ K9        W     E              ◇ J87653
   ♣ J92          S                 ♣ 10
                      ♠ AJ
                      ♡ AK1032
                      ◇ AQ
                      ♣ Q876
```

Contract 3NT by South. Lead ♠K.

The Chief Stoat led the ♠K. Toad spent two minutes counting his winners and another two minutes recounting them. Amazingly the total came to nine both times, so he began to plan for a glorious overtrick.

"He'll go down for sure," thought the Badger, who was watching. He'll never notice the clubs are blocked, not Toad. All he has to do is duck, take the second spade, cross to dummy's ♣A and discard a small club on one of dummy's losing spades. But he's not the player his father was."

Meanwhile Toad was composing his own victory song.

> "The nasty Stoats and Weasels
> Were driven to their knees,
> As they became the victims
> Of Toad's tremendous squeeze."

"That's it," he thought. "I'll bring off one of those suicide squeezes Ratty's always going on about. You let the defence take four tricks and you end up making the next ten."

He took the first trick with the ♠A and immediately played the ♠J. It never occurred to him that West might have led from a six card suit. The Chief Stoat reeled off four spade winners, and Toad discarded from his hand two hearts and, after pulling out the ♡10 and pushing it back again, a club!

"Very clever, Toad, old chap," said the Rat. "I think," he added under his breath.

"Did I make an overtrick?" asked the Toad.

"No," replied the Rat, "But you made your contract."

"It was a suicide squeeze," said the Toad, proudly.

"Actually it was an unblocking play."

"Was it?" The Toad looked glum, then recovered. "I'll have to change my victory song," he said.

> "The nasty Stoats and Weasels
> Will ever rue the day
> When they became the victims
> Of Toad's unblocking play."

The Badger said nothing. He was grateful for small mercies. The Toad had made nine tricks without uttering a single poop.

18
FRANZ KAFKA

A bridge magazine set its readers a difficult problem called 'The Whitfield Six', after the Cambridge don who devised it. A special prize was awarded to a reader who submitted, instead of a solution, a reference to a line from a Shakespeare play. The editor consulted his Complete Works of Shakespeare *and discovered that the line in question was 'I cannot do this bloody thing'.*

Had the great novelist, Franz Kafka, written about bridge, maddening puzzles like this would have suited his style admirably. It was said that he was not so much a writer as an atmosphere. His fiction was precariously balanced between this world and the realm of nightmare. To his central character, 'K', life was an eternal double-dummy problem, with the solution tantalisingly out of reach.

K at the Bridge Club

K walked nervously up the staircase which he had been told led to the bridge club. He found himself in a corridor, and went forward, doubtfully, to its inevitable end.

In the quarter light, he could just make out a heavy, barred door with a small desk at either side. Neither of the two men who sat at the table noticed him. He waited politely for several hours, until plucking up his courage, he coughed discreetly. Receiving no response, he coughed again.

One of the men looked up. "Who are you?" he asked. "No, don't answer that. Tell me what you want and then I can decide whether it's worth finding out who you are."

K fiddled with the brim of his hat. "I was hoping to be allowed to join the bridge club."

"Why?" the man asked. "Do you think that because we are bridge players we can cure your cough? If so you are quite mistaken."

The second man stared at K, his expression both indifferent and hostile. "You realise that you would have to play a rubber so that your play can be assessed?"

"But only members can play a rubber," the first man added. "And you are not a member."

"Besides," said the second man. "You refused to give your name."

"I did not," said K. "My name, as matter of fact, is K."

"Does that stand for Kaplan, or Kantar, or Koch?" asked the two men in unison.

"None of those," replied K.

"Then you will find the standard far too high," said the first man.

"And anyway," said the second man. "There is the paradox."

In a flash, K understood. "You mean that an audition is necessary, but only existing members can audition?"

"Yes. There is, however an alternative. Do you do bridge problems?"

"Yes. That is to say, I try," said K.

"Then try this one," said the second man. He gave K a sheet of paper, and turned his back.

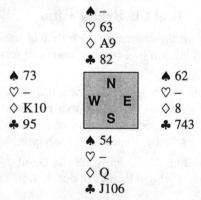

```
              ♠ -
              ♡ 63
              ◇ A9
              ♣ 82
  ♠ 73      ┌─────────┐    ♠ 62
  ♡ -       │    N    │    ♡ -
  ◇ K10     │ W     E │    ◇ 8
  ♣ 95      │    S    │    ♣ 743
            └─────────┘
              ♠ 54
              ♡ -
              ◇ Q
              ♣ J106
```

Hearts are trumps. South to lead and make six tricks.

K stared at the puzzle for a long time. It seemed insoluble. He began to sweat and loosened his collar.

The first man spoke. "You can sleep in the corner if you wish."

"Thank you," said K.

"Not at all. And I will give you a clue. South must not lead a heart."

"He doesn't have a heart," K protested.

"Exactly. That proves the soundness of the clue, doesn't it?"

K stared at the hand again. Then, incredibly, the solution came to him. Frantically, he wrote it in the margin of the paper:

1. South cashes the ♣J playing the ♣8 from dummy.
2. He leads the ♠5 and ruffs with the ♡3.
3. He leads the ♡6 from dummy, discarding the ◊Q. East must discard a diamond, West a spade.
4. The ◊A is led from dummy and East is squeezed.

Trembling with excitement, he gave the paper to the first man, who placed it carefully in a brown envelope.

"But aren't you going to read it?" said K.

"It's not up to us," said the second man. "It must be submitted to the next Annual General Meeting."

"And when is that?" K almost shrieked.

"We do not know, but the last one was yesterday."

The two men turned away, and K walked wearily along the corridor and down the staircase. He realised that he had left his hat behind, but decided not to go back for it.

There was always the Chess Club.

19
THE MASTER

It is a great pity that Sir Noël Coward, 'The Master', did not write about bridge. He was in his prime as a writer during the contract craze of the Thirties, when the game was played in select clubs and Mayfair houses. He could have composed songs like 'Don't Let Your Daughter take up Bridge, Mrs Worthington' and 'Mad Dogs and Englishmen Pre-empt on a Five-Card Suit'.

Some of his insults "She showed all the restraint and good temper of a newly caged cobra" and "He was completely unspoilt by failure" can be aptly applied to several bridge personalities. And it is easy to imagine him, while playing bridge for England, being asked during a rest period whether he is going to watch VuGraph, and replying, "One doesn't watch VuGraph. One appears on it."

Private Lives

Scene: The balcony of a fashionable penthouse flat. Amanda reclines on a sofa. Elyot enters, silently moves behind her and covers her eyes with his hands.

Amanda: Darling, I'd know that touch anywhere.

(*Then disappointed*) Oh, it's you Elyot. I thought you were at the club.

Elyot: I was. I made a divinely improbable three no trumps.

Amanda: Again darling? I wonder why you always lose so heavily?

Elyot: Bridge is an art, not a business.

Amanda: And you are an artist.

Elyot: Not a grocer.

(He opens a bottle of champagne, narrowly missing her with the flying cork)

Amanda: Careful! You just missed me.

Elyot: I know. I really must practise more. Shall I tell you the hand?

Amanda: *(Yawning)* I can't wait.

Elyot: I held ♠A654 ♡K4 ◇AK74 ♣A83. An eighteen point Norfolk.

Amanda: What is a Norfolk?

Elyot: Rather flat. I opened 1◇, 1♡ from partner, 2NT from me.
After an excruciating pause, she bid an agonised 3♡.

Amanda: A sign-off.

Elyot: Absolutely.

Amanda: So you went 3NT?

Elyot: In sleep.

Amanda: God! Who was she?

Elyot: Lady Trumpington.

Amanda: Mayfair's leading underbidder.

Elyot: And underplayer. I scented danger.

Amanda: She might play the contract?

Elyot: Precisely. I bid 3NT in a tone of utter finality.

Amanda: That's what I love about you, Elyot. You're so utterly, utterly,
unselfish.

Elyot: Sarcasm does nothing for you, Amanda.

Amanda: In that respect, it's a little like you my sweet.

Elyot: Charlie Templeton led the ♠J.

Amanda: Dear Charles. Was he there?

Elyot: No, he sent it by carrier pigeon.

Amanda: Did you give him my love?

Elyot: You've given it to him so many times that the offer would have
been superfluous. And then I was confronted with the most
terrible, terrible spectacle.

Amanda: Did the pigeon do something pigeon-like?

Elyot: I was referring to dummy.

Let me show you.

```
                    ♠ 73
                    ♡ AQ10963
                    ◇ J5
                    ♣ Q74
```

```
                    ♠ A654
                    ♡ K4
                    ◇ AK74
                    ♣ A83
```

Amanda: It's a perfectly sweet dummy. You have ten on top.

Elyot: Not with my luck. East was Isobel Carstairs.

Amanda: That horrid vamp. She reminds one of the good time that was had by all.

Elyot: She was bound to hold four hearts to the knave and the ♣K.

Amanda: Why?

Elyot: Life with you, darling, has made me an incorrigible pessimist.

(He writes down the four hands while the audience waits with bated breath)

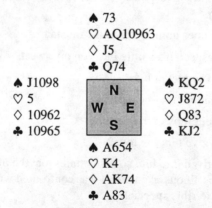

```
                    ♠ 73
                    ♡ AQ10963
                    ◇ J5
                    ♣ Q74
♠ J1098                            ♠ KQ2
♡ 5                                ♡ J872
◇ 10962                            ◇ Q83
♣ 10965                            ♣ KJ2
                    ♠ A654
                    ♡ K4
                    ◇ AK74
                    ♣ A83
```

Amanda: But you said you made the contract. How?

Elyot: I ducked two rounds of spades and took the third, discarding one of dummy's hearts. More champagne?

Amanda: Yes please. Then you led the ♡K, I suppose?

Elyot: No *(smugly)*. The ♡4. And played dummy's ♡9.

Amanda: The ♡9?

Elyot: She did have knave to four.

Amanda: How clever of you.

Elyot: Isobel was equally clever. She executed a very dirty duck.

Amanda: The shameless hussy.

Elyot: It was thoroughly immoral defence.

Amanda: But how did you know Charlie didn't have the ♡J?

Elyot: His tail didn't wag.

Amanda: Poor Charles, he's so damnably emotional. So what did you do?

Elyot: I played the ♡A, felling my own ♡K, then the ♡Q.

Amanda: Your third trick.

Elyot: Then came the coup de grace. The ♡10.

Amanda: I think I see it.

Elyot: Isobel played her ♡J. Her expression was decidedly wan.

Amanda: I'm not surprised. She had no spades.

Elyot: Or hearts.

Amanda: So now she had to lead away from one of her minor suit honours.

Elyot: Giving me an entry to dummy and my ninth trick. Neat?

Amanda: But you were lucky she held all the key cards.

Elyot: Nonsense. It was an unforgettable endplay.

Amanda: What was?

(A pause)

Elyot: My play of ... *(He realises the implication of her question)* Amanda your humour is far too brittle.

Amanda: Incidentally, Master ... could the contract have been set if the Carstairs minx had switched to a heart a trick three?

Elyot: I do not do tragedies. Try Ibsen.

Amanda: But then you could still have made it by -

Elyot: That is intellectual comedy. Try Shaw.

Amanda: But even then ... No, perhaps nothing was of any use.

Elyot: Chekhov.

Amanda: But does it matter? Does anything matter?

Elyot: Beckett.

Amanda: Let's go to bed.

Elyot: Tennessee Williams.

Amanda: Oh, for God's sake shut up!

Elyot: Osborne.

CURTAIN

20
HENRY JAMES

He was a genius to all but a group of his fellow writers. "He had a mind so fine that no idea could disturb it," said T.S. Eliot. "An idiot," wrote H.L. Mencken, "and a Bostonian idiot, to boot, than which there is nothing lower in the world." Mark Twain joined in with, "I would rather be condemned to John Bunyan's heaven than read The Bostonians.*" Oscar Wilde remarked that, "Mr James writes fiction as though it were a painful duty," and wished he had also said, "Mr James does not bite off more than he can chew; he chews more than he can bite off."*

On the other hand, British academicians revere him as one of the truly great English novelists, simultaneously granting him immortality and naturalisation. His masterpiece was probably The Ambassadors, *the story of a man called Strether, despatched to Paris by the virtuous widow, Mrs Newsome, to rescue her son, Chadwick, from the clutches of the Vicomtesse de Viennot – or from whatever else the young scamp had got himself into.*

Strether's secondary objective was, as with all James's characters, to continue the master's search for the mot juste, a quest which would have few nouns unqualified and no phrase unchallenged.

The Ambassador

That Chad Newsome could have come to this, an ignominious surrender to the sensual lure of Auction Bridge, had seemed unthinkable – perhaps even unimaginable – to poor guileless Strether, until he saw with his own incredulous eyes the expression of pure dumb blind rapture with which Chad watched his partner, the beguilingly notorious – or, more accurately, the notoriously beguiling – Vicomtesse put down the dummy.

Strether peered over Chad's shoulder, the better to see the cards of 'declarer' – he was dimly aware of the quaintly inappropriate term – were not 'declarations' often made by dummy, or, since they were delightfully in Paris, *le mort*? He was in a sense – not that any part of his cryptic mission made sense, hang it – Mrs Newsome's ambassador, and she required him to bring back, if not her beloved prodigal son in person, then at least a full account of Chad's depravities, card by card, omitting no titillating details of their denominational characteristics.

The Vicomtesse
♠ 1097
♡ Q
◇ QJ76
♣ A8764

♠ KQ4   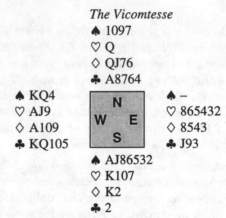   ♠ –
♡ AJ9   ♡ 865432
◇ A109   ◇ 8543
♣ KQ105   ♣ J93

♠ AJ86532
♡ K107
◇ K2
♣ 2

Strether realised with a long-drawn pang of panic that he had missed the deuced bidding – he would have to invent a mendacious but plausible sequence for Mrs Newsome – but he knew that the contract was a rash, bleak, doomed four spades, doubled in a roar of ungentlemanly thunder by Chad's 'left hand opponent', who with paradoxical dexterousness, led the ♣K.

Chad greeted this card with a cry of despair, triumph, surprise or maybe sheer bland bored indifference – Strether could not for the life of him decide which – won 'on the table' and immediately ruffed a club 'in hand'. Then came a low heart, captured by the thunderous doubler, who went into an immediate trance, terminated by the surprising appearance of his ♡9.

Of course this was – or seemed to be – a gift; leading into the grim, wide[1] jaws of declarer's tenace, but Chad spurned it, ruffing in dummy. Another club was trumped and the ◇K led – ducked by the doubling thunderer

---

[1] The reader may query the absence of a third short terse blunt adjective; perhaps this is one of James' daring experiments in style, or, possibly a misprint.

with a look of sheer low animal cunning. Chad continued with the ♡K, trumping in dummy, and ruffed yet another club. 'Exiting' with his last diamond, he had created the following position:

```
              ♠ 10
              ♡ –
              ◇ QJ
              ♣ 6
♠ KQ4       ┌─────────┐
♡ –         │    N    │
◇ 10        │  W   E  │         Utterly Irrelevant
♣ –         │    S    │
            └─────────┘
              ♠ ΛJ86
              ♡ –
              ◇ –
              ♣ –
```

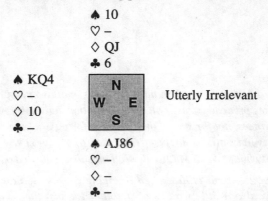

The defence was – there was no other word for it – emasculated[1]. The thubbling dunderer returned the ◇10, but Chad ruffed, and his ♠8 executed a crisp neat trim end-play.

There was nothing to be said, and the Vicomtesse was the first to say it. 'Bien joué!' she cried, in a voice which suggested to Strether that bridge may not have been the only infernal habit which Chad had shamefully yet shamelessly embraced. His next epistle to Mrs Newsome would need to be composed with meticulous care – she would expect something better than a prosaic trump reduction – the bridge books were full of the confounded things – he would have to embellish the hand as well as the bidding.

He concluded he would need twelve reams of writing paper and two and a half litres of ink. But nagging incessantly at his stream of consciousness[2] was the insidious thought – "would that be enough?"

---

[1] Note James' off-hand rejection of the alternative, 'buggered'.

[2] Here he anticipated Virginia Woolf. Perhaps this was why she wrote that "Reading James was like being entombed in black amber."

21
BRIDGE AT ST TITUS

David Bird created the splendidly eccentric monastery of St. Titus, where bridge takes precedence over all other religious activities and postulants are given penances, not for sins of the flesh, but for passing the Abbot's cue bids. St. Titus sends missionaries to Africa, to convert the natives not to Christianity but to Acol. Multi-coloured bids are regarded as major heresies.

The pompous Abbot is described as being greatly jealous of his reputation. He is also a little jealous of Brother Lucius, the monastery accountant, who, unlike his superior, is a genuine Master.

Brother Xavier is the monastery's barber. Brother Paulo is an Italian monk transferred to strengthen the St. Titus team.

The Abbot Bids For Glory

The Abbot's ancient Austin Seven squealed protestingly to a halt outside an imposing Georgian building. Brother Lucius admired the splendour of the architecture, while the Abbot piously hoped that it would be matched by the quality of the refreshments.

St. Titus were playing a team from the Agnostics Club in the fourth round of the Gold Cup. They were greeted somewhat diffidently by the opposing Captain, Ivor Doutt.

"A curiously ironic draw," remarked Ivor. "You could scarcely imagine two sides more diametrically opposed – in our philosophies, I mean."

The Abbot looked concerned. "You play the Strong Pass?" he asked, anxiously. "If so I must point out ... "

"No nothing of the sort." Ivor reassured him. "It's just that, theologically speaking, we maintain that knowledge is limited by human experience."

The Abbot brightened visibly. "Ah! then you play straight Acol. So do we. I look forward to an excellent match."

"I would normally offer you all a small sherry," said Ivor. "But I expect you've given it up for Lent."

"No, this year we've given up weak jump overcalls," replied the Abbot, glancing approvingly at the well-stocked bar. "What excellent glassware. Those large schooners are particularly fine examples."

The Abbot and Brother Xavier played the first half against Ivor and an agnostic called Thomas. After some uneventful boards, the Abbot at last had an opportunity to display his mastery.

Game All. Dealer East.

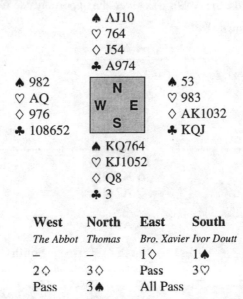

```
                        ♠ AJ10
                        ♡ 764
                        ◇ J54
                        ♣ A974
        ♠ 982          ┌─────────┐        ♠ 53
        ♡ AQ           │    N    │        ♡ 983
        ◇ 976          │  W   E  │        ◇ AK1032
        ♣ 108652       │    S    │        ♣ KQJ
                        └─────────┘
                        ♠ KQ764
                        ♡ KJ1052
                        ◇ Q8
                        ♣ 3
```

West	North	East	South
The Abbot	*Thomas*	*Bro. Xavier*	*Ivor Doutt*
–	–	1◇	1♠
2◇	3◇	Pass	3♡
Pass	3♠	All Pass	

The Abbot sensed that his opponents had bid conservatively. An attacking lead was called for. He recalled a similar situation from his treatise on opening leads and laid down the ♡A, which he hoped had every appearance of a singleton. He continued with the ◇9. Brother Xavier won with the ◇K and returned the ♡9. If declarer took the 'marked' finesse, the Abbot would win with the ♡Q, put his partner in with the ◇A and obtain his well earned heart ruff to set the contract. He was already anticipating the admiration of the novices as he recounted the brilliancy.

Ivor looked sceptically at the ♡9. Eventually, he rose with the ♡K and made his contract with an overtrick.

"Amazing," said the Abbot, trying unsuccessfully to disguise his irritation. "May I ask why you didn't read my ♡A as a singleton?"

"But I did, Abbot," replied Ivor. "However, had it been singleton I would have been down anyway. My only hope was that you were expert enough to choose such a remarkable deception, rather than the ... er ... successful alternative. I am glad my faith was not misplaced."

In the other room, Brother Lucius and Brother Paulo reached a more adventurous 4♠. The prosaic diamond lead was followed by a heart switch. West cashed both heart winners and returned a diamond so that East could give him his heart ruff and set the contract by two tricks.

Soon afterwards, the Abbot was given the opportunity to redeem himself.

Game All. Dealer West.

♠ AQJ
♡ K85
◇ AJ73
♣ J62

♠ K10953
♡ A743
◇ 2
♣ AK5

West	North	East	South
Thomas	*Bro. Xavier*	*Ivor Doutt*	*The Abbot*
Pass	1◇	Pass	1♠
Pass	1NT(i)	Pass	2♣(ii)
Pass	3♠	Pass	4♣
Pass	4◇	Pass	4♡
Pass	5♡	Pass	6♠
All Pass			

(i)   12-16 points
(ii) Asking for range and shape

The king of diamonds was led and the Abbot surveyed the dummy with distaste. There appeared to be eleven winners including a possible heart ruff. His first idea was to ruff a diamond and play a club towards dummy, hoping to get past West's queen. Then a better plan occurred to him. Trumping a diamond at trick two, he crossed twice to dummy's ♠QJ and ruffed out the remaining diamonds, which proved to be 4-4. Crossing to the ♡K, he reached the following position:

```
            ♠ A
            ♡ 85
            ◇ -
            ♣ J62
```

```
            ♠ -
            ♡ A74
            ◇ -
            ♣ AK5
```

On the lead of the ♠A, East threw the ♣4, and the Abbot had to find a discard. Deciding to play East for an original holding of four hearts and three clubs to the queen, he threw a heart and laid down the ♣AK, felling East's ♣Q. The full deal was:

```
                    ♠ AQJ
                    ♡ K85
                    ◇ AJ73
                    ♣ J62
    ♠ 864                        ♠ 72
    ♡ J6                         ♡ Q1092
    ◇ KQ109                      ◇ 8654
    ♣ 9873                       ♣ Q104
                    ♠ K10953
                    ♡ A743
                    ◇ 2
                    ♣ AK5
```

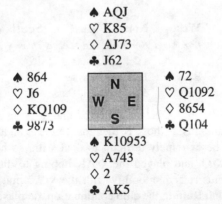

"That was fortunate, Abbot," said Brother Xavier. "You might have played for hearts to be 3-3, rather than for East to have that specific holding."

"Some players might have said, well played, after seeing a dummy reversal and squeeze without the count," said the Abbot in sepulchral tones. Perhaps he could use the hand in his sermon following day. Yes, he could put it after that instructive mistake that Lucius had made in the last league match.

"I would also point out," he added, "that a top class declarer takes into account not just the percentages but the tempo of the discards. The fact that the line I chose was more spectacular did not enter my considerations."

East had in fact discarded a club smoothly but he let the Abbot's remark pass without comment.

In the second half, Brother Lucius and Brother Paulo faced Ivor and Thomas.

North/South Game. Dealer North.

```
                    ♠ J65
                    ♡ KQ8
                    ◊ AKJ5
                    ♣ 762
    ♠ Q74                          ♠ 983
    ♡ 54           N               ♡ AJ9
    ◊ 109832    W     E            ◊ 64
    ♣ QJ9          S               ♣ K10943
                    ♠ AK102
                    ♡ 107632
                    ◊ Q7
                    ♣ A5
```

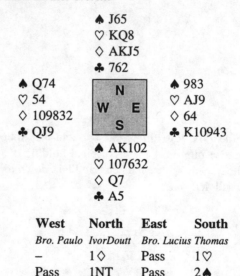

West	North	East	South
Bro. Paulo	*IvorDoutt*	*Bro. Lucius*	*Thomas*
–	1◊	Pass	1♡
Pass	1NT	Pass	2♠
Pass	4♡	All Pass	

Brother Paulo led the ♣Q. Declarer reflected that ducking risked an immediate switch to diamonds. If the ♡K then lost to the ♡A, another diamond from East would be extremely difficult to deal with, so he won with the ♣A, cashed the ◊Q, and played the ◊AK hoping to discard his losing club. Brother Lucius ruffed smoothly with the ♡9, upon which Thomas threw his losing club.Ruffing the club continuation, he played a heart to the king, taken by Brother Lucius, who returned another club, again ruffed by declarer.

The position was now:

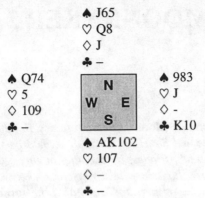

```
              ♠ J65
              ♡ Q8
              ◇ J
              ♣ –
  ♠ Q74                    ♠ 983
  ♡ 5         N            ♡ J
  ◇ 109    W     E         ◇ -
  ♣ –         S            ♣ K10
              ♠ AK102
              ♡ 107
              ◇ –
              ♣ –
```

Thomas was now at the crossroads. He reviewed the play so far. East he now knew to be a formidable performer, quite capable of playing the ♡9 from ♡AJ9 without a flicker. Eventually he decided that an original ♡A9 was more likely, if only because, had he held the jack, East might have played it. Thomas led a heart and put in dummy's ♡8. The loss of a spade was by now unavoidable and the contract was one down.

"A pretty defence," said Ivor. "If you discard on the third round of diamonds or ruff with the ♡J Thomas gets rid of his club loser, and nothing can stop him making the contract. I hope our other pair defend as cleverly."

Brother Lucius smiled to himself. "If they do," he thought, "the Abbot will describe it as an automatic play."

In the other room, the Abbot ducked the opening club lead and settled for the loss of one club and two hearts, discarding his losing spades on dummy's diamond winners.

After the match, Ivor Doutt offered the Monastery team a final sherry, and congratulated them on their victory. "I think board 39 was the turning point of an excellent match," he said.

The Abbot looked pleased. "You mean my duck of the ♣A?"

"No, it was the burst of thunder and lightning that accompanied my failure to switch to diamonds at trick two," replied Ivor. "I almost wished we could call up reinforcements like that."

22
MOONRAKER 2

It was in Ian Fleming's Moonraker *that James Bond won his famous bridge duel with the evil Sir Hugh Drax. Drax had been desecrating the august gentleman's club, Blades, by cheating at cards. Compared to this his attempt to destroy London with a nuclear rocket was a mild misdemeanour. Fortunately, or perhaps inevitably, he turned out not to be British, but, like all of Bond's adversaries, an unprincipled foreigner.*

Bridge-playing Bond fans lamented the omission of the great bridge scene from the film, which included in its stead a tasteful episode in which one of the heroines was devoured by two .... No, it's too awful for gentle, peace-loving bridge players to think about.

For Your Mind Only

"If you've finished harassing my secretary, 007, I'd like a word with you."

James Bond felt his muscles go taut with anticipation. M called him by his number only when he was about to give him a dangerous assignment. He helped Miss Moneypenny to her feet and entered his chief's office.

"What are you doing at the moment?" asked M.

"Well sir, there's a Spectre plot to kidnap the Queen."

"Never mind about that. Something's happened which could destroy civilisation as we know it. Blades have another member who cheats at bridge."

Bond's eyes narrowed. He really would have to see an optician soon. "Really sir? I thought we'd put a stop to that when I exposed Drax?"

"Evidently not. And debagging won't work with this chap. His name's Karduni. He heads a syndicate which controls half the oil in the Gulf. The Foreign Office say we can't touch him."

"Did you tell the F.O. that the Service puts Blades before the Gulf?"

"Of course."

"And what did they say sir?"

"F.O."

"I see," said Bond. "Tell me sir. How do you know the fellow cheats?"

"He has won sixty consecutive rubbers."

"Who against?"

"Zia, Irving, Martin, Andrew, Omar ... "

Bond frowned. "How does he do it sir? Shiners? Marked cards?"

M shook his head. "No, we've had experts watching his every move." He stood up, abruptly. "Come on 007. We've got to get there for the first rubber of the evening."

Ten minutes later, they arrived at Blades and went into the famous card room, where a rubber was just beginning. They ordered a bottle of Krug and sat down to watch the play.

Karduni was a dark, middle aged man of medium height, yet as Bond studied him he became aware of something very strange. Unlike any villain he had met during his fifty-five years with Naval Intelligence, the oil tycoon had no eccentricity whatsoever. He was utterly colourless. When they filmed this episode, Bond thought, they would never get a reputable actor to take his part.

He never spoke, except to bid. His concentration was intense, his bids and plays inspired. Zia, Irving, Martin, Andrew and Omar were all dazzled by his miraculous card reading.

Then, suddenly, Bond found the answer staring him in the face. He gave M a secret signal and they retired to the elegant dining room.

Bond explained his theory between mouthfuls of caviare and pre-war Wolfschmidt. "You'll probably think I'm a raving lunatic, sir."

"Not you, James," his chief smiled. "You've saved the world far too often."

"I believe Karduni is a mind reader."

"You must be a raving lunatic!"

"It's the only possible explanation sir. When you had to leave the room, he played a hand brilliantly, but hopelessly against the odds."

He wrote out four hands:

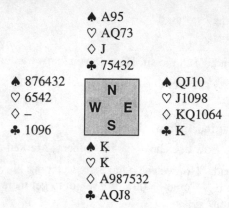

```
                ♠ A95
                ♡ AQ73
                ◇ J
                ♣ 75432
♠ 876432                    ♠ QJ10
♡ 6542        N            ♡ J1098
◇ -        W     E         ◇ KQ1064
♣ 1096        S            ♣ K
                ♠ K
                ♡ K
                ◇ A987532
                ♣ AQJ8
```

"Karduni was South, in a wild six no trumps. The ♠8 was led. How would you play, sir?"

M looked at the seemingly impossible contract. "Under an assumed name," he smiled.

Bond regarded him impassively and wondered whether his disinclination to laugh at old jokes was the reason why he had remained a lieutenant commander for more than three decades. "Well Karduni played, the ♡K, then the ♣A, dropping the singleton king."

"Astounding!"

"There's more to come. He now played the ♣Q and the ♣8!"

"But why?"

"West had to take and lead a major. Karduni took the trick in dummy, led the ♡A and unblocked his ♣J. Then he reeled off the clubs subjecting East to a progressive squeeze." [1]

"Incredible. What did Zia say?"

"He couldn't say much. He does things like that all the time."

M sighed and lit a cheroot. "I'm convinced. Karduni reads minds. What now?"

A faint smile appeared on Bond's hard, cruel mouth. A waitress swooned with desire. Another dropped a plate. "We give him such a beating that he'll never play again."

"But he'll know what you're going to do before you do it."

---

[1] Hand is from *Bridge: The Ultimate Limits* by Mansfield

"I realise that, sir. I'll have to get so drunk that my mind becomes an unreadable mess, so if you'll just order a few bottles of Taylor's '47 ...."

Two litres later, he felt ready for what he had to do. His mind was reeling with so many alcoholic thoughts that he was confident that no mind-reader would pick out the single notion that in his breast pocket were two stacked decks, one red and one blue.

He staggered into the card room just in time to join Karduni's game. He cut Basildon, the club secretary, against an ageing general and Karduni, who sat at his right and dealt the first hand.

Bond's luck was in. Nothing could stop them bidding six spades, which Basildon made easily. Karduni cut the pack to Bond for the next deal. Their eyes met, and Bond gasped mentally as a diamond sharp thought invaded his mind. The man was not just a receiver, he was a sender!

"You are James Bond?" the thought asked. "Also known as 007?"

"You can read my mind!" Bond thought back, feigning incredulity.

"Not fully. You are so disgustingly drunk that it does not make pleasant reading. But I recognised you from your photographs."

"What photographs?"

"I am a member of Spectre."

"And you dare admit it?"

"Of course. I've been waiting for you to turn up, Mr. Bond. I wanted to meet you."

"Really? How is your latest plot progressing?"

"Which one?"

"The little matter of kidnapping Her Majesty."

"Ah yes." The thought came through as a knowing smile. "We guessed you knew about that. I 'm here to offer you a deal."

"We won't deal with Spectre."

"Surely you did on one occasion?"

"No. That was SMERSH."

Bond looked at the other players. Neither realised what was happening. The entire uncanny mental exchange had taken only a few seconds. The wine waiter arrived with a bottle of Dom Perignon, a diversion from M to cover Bond's next move. Forcing his mind on other things, he quickly switched packs and dealt the following carefully prepared hands:

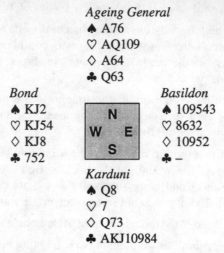

Ageing General
♠ A76
♡ AQ109
◇ A64
♣ Q63

Bond
♠ KJ2
♡ KJ54
◇ KJ8
♣ 752

Basildon
♠ 109543
♡ 8632
◇ 10952
♣ –

Karduni
♠ Q8
♡ 7
◇ Q73
♣ AKJ10984

Bond focused drunkenly on his twelve points and nothing else. As he expected, Karduni, sitting South, reached the improbable 7♣. On the book lead of a small club, the grand slam would be ice cold. Declarer unblocks the ♠A and the ◇A, a double Vienna coup, and runs off clubs, leaving:

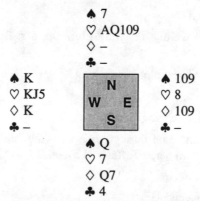

♠ 7
♡ AQ109
◇ –
♣ –

♠ K
♡ KJ5
◇ K
♣ –

♠ 109
♡ 8
◇ 109
♣ –

♠ Q
♡ 7
◇ Q7
♣ 4

The lead of the last club begins a deadly progressive squeeze against West, and Bond already knew the man's flair for progressive squeezes.

The mind-reader's next thought intruded on a port-induced fantasy about Pussy Galore. "Suppose we bet on the outcome of this hand. If I make my contract, Mr. Bond, you let us have the Queen. If I lose, we will give your country three Arab Emirates."

"You expect me to agree to a deal like that?"

"Yes."

"All right. Make it four Emirates. And you give up playing at Blades."

"Agreed, Mr. Bond. Provided you throw in Prince Charles."

"And you must return the money you've won from Zia, Irving, Martin ...."

"Yes, yes, yes!"

"But how do I know we can trust you?" asked Bond trying to infuse an alcoholic hiccup into the thought.

"I have never broken my word, Mr. Bond."

"You cheat at cards." Bond's accusation oozed contempt.

"I refer you to the Laws of Contract Bridge. They forbid drawing illicit inferences from various sources, but mind-reading is not specified."

Bond smiled. The man had a point. "You're on," he said, and led, not the safe club but ♡K!

Karduni stared at the card in astonishment. Zia who was watching, made a frantic note. "I wish I'd played that, " he said wistfully.

"You will Zia, you will, " replied Bond.

Karduni did his best, by playing off his clubs, but the last seven cards were:

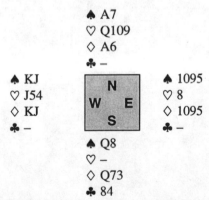

On the next club lead, James discarded the ♡4. Karduni considered every possibility. There was no way to avoid a loser, barring a defensive error, and Bond had no intention of making one.

He opened his mind fully to his opponent, and sensed the bitter thought, "Congratulations. I underrated you."

"So did Doctor No, Goldfinger, Blofeld and Scaramanga. But you'll keep your word?"

"About the Queen, yes." Karduni rose, and as he left Blades for the last time, he flashed a final thought to his adversary. "But if I were you, Mr. Bond, I would start locking my door at nights."

Bond said nothing. His mind was focused on a tantalising dilemma. Should he have the waitress who swooned, or the one who dropped the plate?

23
LEWIS CARROLL

Lewis Carroll is a natural subject for a bridge parody. A great many of his poems were themselves parodies of other works, so he had an eye (or ear) for forms which lent themselves to burlesque.

He was a distinguished mathematician who was fascinated by puzzles and games like chess and cards. He was also an indefatigable children's entertainer. One afternoon, he arrived at an 'at home' and, as was his habit, made straight for the room which had been set aside for the guests' children. He covered his head and shoulders with an overcoat and, pretending that one of its loose arms was a trunk, entered on all fours in his celebrated impersonation of an elephant. Surprised not to be greeted by the usual squeals of laughter, he took off the overcoat and found he was in a room full of grown ups.

And as Michael Caine would say, "Not a lot of people know that".

Silence in Court

The other day she played with you,
Opposing him and me.
You opened with a forcing two,
And heard her give you three
You trotted out the good old Black,
And found her with an ace.
Since you had four, you settled back,
A smile upon your face.
To five no trumps, her swift reply
Revealed she held two kings,
And you had three, and gave a sigh –
Pigs really did have wings!
With great aplomb, you bid the grand.
She promptly raised to eight!
A knave and four queens in your hand
Meant nine was on a plate.
But he and I then sprang to life,
And doubled you and she.
For after all you were my wife,
And she was Mrs He.
The fact that you went fourteen off
Both he and I thought sad,
For she was tired, you had a cough,
And both of you were mad.
And we were playing with five suits,
The fifth one being green,
And he and I were in cahoots,
And he had all thirteen.
So next time that she partners you,
On some capricious whim,
The one thing you must never do
Is play with me and him.

Father William

"You are old Father William," the young man said,
"And while I don't wish to be rude,
Although you can put a tough contract to bed,
Your bidding is terribly crude."

"In my youth," Father William replied to his son,
"I learned that it pays to be bold.
And blitzing to game is my notion of fun,
And nobody knows what I hold."

"You are old," said the youth, "and I've frequently seen
That your vulnerable no trump is light.
I wish you'd stop opening on twelve to fourteen,
Lest they double you clean out of sight."

"When young," said the old man, repressing a snore,
"I decided that bridge was a giggle.
And if my opponents are quick on the draw,
There's always the Rimington Wriggle."

"You are old, Father William," the young man cried,
"And of science your bridge bears no traces.
And when you bid slams it's a blow to my pride
That you don't ever ask me for Aces."

"In the days of my youth." Father William intoned,
"I was fond of the works of James Thurber,
Who taught me that bridge was more fun when you're stoned,
And can't cope with Blackwood and Gerber."

"But you're old, Father William!" the boy did persist,
"And your hair is old-fashioned and thinning.
And you bid every hand as though partially pissed.
I can't fathom why you keep winning."

"I've answered your questions." His father was gruff.
"And I'm going to lodge an appeal.
I don't want to listen all day to this stuff,
So sit down, and shut up and deal!"

The Duchess's Lullaby

Speak roughly to your little boy,
And beat him when he squeezes.
He only rectifies the count,
Because he knows it teases.

I speak severely to my boy,
And beat him when he squeezes,
For he can thoroughly enjoy
Finessing when he pleases.

The Walrus and The Hog

"The time has come,'" the Walrus said,
"To talk of many things.
Are jacks and queens worth one and two,
With three full points for kings?"

"I recommend," the Hog replied,
"When I'm to play the hand,
You add a point for twos and threes.
I'm sure you'll understand."

24
RIGHT THROUGH THE PACK

Described as 'a bridge fantasy', this classic by Robert Darvas and Norman de V. Hart contains fifty two remarkable hands, one for every card in the pack. Each hand is part of a story and the stories are told by each card in turn.

Right Through the Pack *was first published in 1947, so today's reader must be prepared to accept the social conventions of the period. The Tens are the minor aristocrats of the pack. As honour cards, they are usually thrusting for promotion, but the Ten of Hearts, perhaps through so often being placed next to the dashing Knave, had acquired some of that prince's flair for romance.*

A Cool Deception
(The Tale of The Ten of Hearts)

Charles and Susan were hopelessly in love. She was the only child of a millionaire, recently ennobled for his success in the City. Charles was the second son of a penniless Earl. He could trace his ancestry to Plantagenet Kings, and his poverty to a forbear who had lost the family fortune on a single hand of Whist. A humble classics scholar, Charles was clearly not a fit suitor for a girl who would one day inherit a vast business.

The Baron had three passions: his financial empire, his daughter and bridge. Every Saturday at his country home, he would entertain three of his friends to a splendid dinner, followed by some friendly rubbers.

On one such evening, a guest had dined so well, and so unwisely, that an attack of indigestion had forced him to retire early. The Baron walked disconsolately into the library, where Charles was reading Sophocles to an adoring Susan.

"Oh you're here," said the Baron gruffly. "I don't suppose you play bridge, do you?"

"As a matter of fact I do, sir."

"You astound me. Well, Euripides, you can put down that Greek nonsense and make up a four. It will give me the chance to see what you're made of. Don't worry, I'll stand your losses."

Charles found himself partnering the Baron against a bookmaker and a scrap metal merchant, both knighted for their contributions to the Arts. I could sense his nervousness as he sorted his cards, placing me next to my leader, the Ace. Susan sat on his left, and the Ace agreed with me that somehow they both knew their whole future could depend upon this single hand.

Love All. Dealer South.

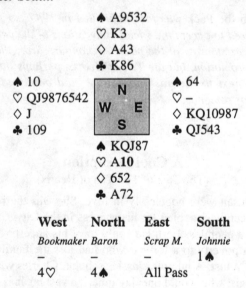

```
                 ♠ A9532
                 ♡ K3
                 ◇ A43
                 ♣ K86
  ♠ 10                          ♠ 64
  ♡ QJ9876542     N             ♡ –
  ◇ J          W     E          ◇ KQ10987
  ♣ 109           S             ♣ QJ543
                 ♠ KQJ87
                 ♡ A10
                 ◇ 652
                 ♣ A72
```

West	North	East	South
Bookmaker	*Baron*	*Scrap M.*	*Johnnie*
–	–	–	1♠
4♡	4♠	All Pass	

Contract 4♠ by South. The ♡Q led.

Charles played the ♡K from dummy and was resigned when the scrap merchant ruffed. The cruel duplication meant that there were only nine winners. Then Charles realised that this was almost a replica of a famous hand, in which dealer held not the ♡A10 but the ♡A2.

The play with the latter combination is striking. Declarer must throw his ♡A on the first trick! Whatever East plays, he wins, draws trumps and plays the ♣AK and the ◇A, stripping West.

The remaining cards are:

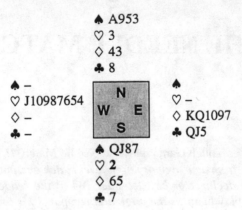

                    ♠ A953
                    ♡ 3
                    ◇ 43
                    ♣ 8

    ♠ —   ♠
    ♡ J10987654   N   E   ♡ —
    ◇ —   W   E   ◇ KQ1097
    ♣ —   S   ♣ QJ5

                    ♠ QJ87
                    ♡ 2
                    ◇ 65
                    ♣ 7

At trick six, declarer leads his carefully preserved ♡2, forcing West to win. On the heart lead a diamond is thrown from hand and a club from dummy. On the next heart, declarer ruffs in dummy and discards his last diamond, making a spectacular contract. But, alas, I was not a humble deuce; my rank would enable the bookmaker to duck at trick six. This would be fine play, but he would surely be forewarned by declarer's jettison of the ♡A.

All this went through Charles' mind before he played from hand to trick one. Contriving to appear devastated by East's ruff, he dropped the ♡A and reacted as though it was a catastrophic misplay. So when he led me at trick six, with a sheepish air, West covered with the ♡J, and was forced to give declarer the ruff and three discards ....

As the Ten paused in his narrative, there was a shocked silence, finally broken by the angry Queen of Hearts. "We are not amused," she announced. "That you should have been party to such a roguish deception is bad enough; what is far worse is that you seem to approve of it."

"Your majesty, my tale is not yet finished," the Ten replied. "Having proved that he could make the contract, Charles gaily played out all the trumps, spurning the elementary cross ruff and finishing in his hand. When he led the ♣7 at trick thirteen, it lost to East's ♣Q."

The pack applauded with admiration and relief. "A magnificent gesture," pronounced the King. "He quixotically snatched defeat from the jaws of victory. What was the Baron's reaction?"

"He was overwhelmed, your Majesty. He said that he had never before seen skill, daring, deception and integrity displayed in a single hand. He welcomed Charles as a son-in-law and partner in his business."

25
THE NEEDLE MATCH

In his books, The Tough Game *and* The Needle Match, *H.W. Kelsey presents the hands from an imaginary high level match and puts the reader in the position of declarer or key defender. When the reader has decided how he would play he turns the page and compares his line with the one recommended. He also learns what happened in the other room, and the knowledge is often salutary.*

The hands are interesting and instructive, but most players will need to be on their best form to finish on the winning side.

As you will see . . .

Problem

North/South Game. Dealer South.

♠ AQ94
♡ AK6
◇ 73
♣ 10763

♠ KJ8
♡ Q8
◇ A52
♣ AK984

West	North	East	South
–	–	–	1♣
Pass	1♠	Pass	2NT
Pass	3♣	Pass	3◇
Pass	3♡	Pass	3♠
Pass	4♡	Pass	4NT
Pass	5♡	Pass	6♣
All Pass			

You reach a rather optimistic contract of 6♣. The ◇K is led. You win in hand, lay down the ♣AK and find that West began with the ♣QJ5.

How do you continue?

Solution

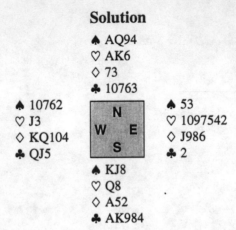

```
              ♠ AQ94
              ♡ AK6
              ◇ 73
              ♣ 10763
♠ 10762                      ♠ 53
♡ J3            N            ♡ 1097542
◇ KQ104     W     E          ◇ J986
♣ QJ5          S             ♣ 2
              ♠ KJ8
              ♡ Q8
              ◇ A52
              ♣ AK984
```

Clearly you must hope to discard your losing diamonds on dummy's major suit winners, and it may seem right to begin with hearts, as there is less chance that you will suffer a ruff. As the cards lie, this line will fail as West will trump the third round and cash his ◇ K.

In fact you should have reasoned that you cannot succeed unless West has at least three spades, so you may as well give yourself an extra chance by playing spades first. As the cards lie, East shows out on the third round, you discard one diamond loser on the fourth spade, and the other on the third round of hearts. Whether West ruffs or not, you will now make your twelve tricks.

In the other room, East opened a sub-minimum multi-2 ◇, which persuaded West to double 6♣. South redoubled, and found the correct line, making a surprise overtrick when East revoked.

So if you played hearts first you lose 19 IMPs. If you correctly started with spades you hold the loss to a mere 13 IMPs.

Tough.

26
THE WINNING EDGE

Jeremy Flint, co-author of Tiger Bridge *and author of* The Winning Edge, *was a Renaissance Man. He was inclined to begin an article with a dissertation on cricket or chess, leaving his readers wondering which bridge theme it would introduce.*

An example of his discursive style might have been:

> *The ship of Theseus sailed the Mediterranean for many years. Every day, a piece of timber was thrown overboard and replaced, until no original part of the ship remained. By chance, all the discarded pieces were washed to the shore of an Aegean island, where a shipwright collected them and built a perfect replica of Theseus' vessel. Which was now the ship of Theseus?*

Instantly, you would guess that this is analogous to the history of the Acol system, each original principle having been replaced over time by the Baron 2NT, Benjamin two bids, fourth suit forcing, Blackwood and so on. If an enterprising pair were to rediscover and license the ideas of Marx and Simon, which would now be the Acol system?

The next piece deals with a different branch of bridge philosophy.

The Whole Truth

Among my favourite problems is one which might have been devised by Wittgenstein. Imagine that you have a choice of two roads, but no way of determining which of them leads to London. Fortunately you meet two brothers, one an inveterate and consistent liar, the other invariably truthful. Both know the right road, but because of the perverse rules which apply to intelligence tests but to no other aspect of life, you may pose only one question to one brother. Was there anything else? Oh yes. You have no means of knowing which brother is which, so you must devise a question that will elicit the same answer from either.

I was in a similar situation in Juan les Pins, playing with Tony Priday against the brothers Stankovic, leading Bulgarian internationals, but unrelated to the novelist my readers are doubtless familiar with. I sat South:

♠ Q72
♡ Q54
♢ 542
♣ KQJ2

♠ AJ10964
♡ A32
♢ AKQ
♣ A

Our opponents were playing a Strong Pass, which led to a somewhat bizarre auction.

West	North	East	South
V. St'vic	*Priday*	*Z. St'vic*	*Flint*
1♠	Pass	1NT	Dble
Rdble	Pass	2♣	3♣
Pass	3NT	Pass	4♠
Pass	5♠	Pass	6♠
All Pass			

The opening 1♠ showed 0-8 points and West had either 0-2 or 5+ spades. Yes, there really are systems like that.

The ♣10 was led, East following with the ♣3. I took in hand and wondered how best to reach dummy. I was already at the crossroads, faced with the question – which brother held the ♠K? If I led towards the ♠Q and found East with something like the ♠K85. I would have to endure Tony's good-natured sympathy.

Then I hit upon a neat, if slightly risky solution. East's play of the ♣3 suggested that clubs were 5-3. West's redouble suggested he had 0-2 spades and support for the other suits. Did this mean that diamonds were going to break nicely, or that the Stankovics were mendacious Bulgars? I decided to trust them and led the ♢AKQ, hoping for a 4-3 split or that the brother with the doubleton held the ♠K, singleton or once guarded.

When both defenders followed to three rounds, I led the ♠J and overtook with the ♠Q. If Z. Stankovic ducked I would be in dummy to enjoy the winning clubs. If he took with the ♠K, whatever he led would create an entry to the table.

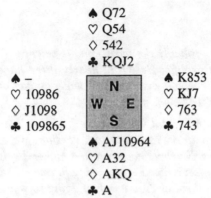

On reflection, I am not sure that the line I chose was mathematically the best, but aesthetically it is unchallengeable.

To return to the crossroads problem, the solution is that you point a gun randomly to one of the roads and one of the brothers and say, "If I asked your brother whether that road leads to London, what would he reply?" If you happen to have pointed to the wrong road, each brother will give an affirmative response, and vice versa.

If you are ever in that situation, I hope you find this useful.

Next week, I will deal with the subject of how to play a contract when the adverse trumps break 8-5.

27
MASTER OF SCI FI

Isaac Asimov was probably the most famous science fiction writer, and certainly the most prolific. He wrote nearly three hundred books, and when asked what he would wish for if he knew he had only three months to live, he replied, "To type faster".

Perhaps his most important works were his novels about robots and androids (the humaniform variety). Both versions were primed to obey several robotic laws. No robot could harm a human being. All robots had a compulsion to protect a human from being harmed. They were also programmed to protect themselves, but only if doing so would not contravene the first two laws. Being a robot was not always a bed of roses.

The development of computers and the feasibility of a robot society have already helped us to understand the nature of logical thought, as opposed to creativity, flair and instinct. If humans possess these latter qualities, does this mean they will always be mentally superior to robots? Or can the so-called intuitive process be analysed and programmed into a computer?

In other words, could a bridge playing computer have flair?

Flair

Jord Nomash savoured his 2262 château-bottled Auroran Sauvignon.

"I agree that a robot could play a sound game," he said. "Perfect counting, memory, calculation. Nevertheless ..."

"No flair?" Par Dallow smiled. "Yes, I know you contend that bridge requires that nebulous quality."

"I've watched you play, my friend." Nomash raised his glass in salute, hoping his host would notice it was empty. "Some of your coups defy the odds, yet they work."

"And you call that flair?"

"The Dictionary Galactica does it for me. 'The innate propensity to perform effective actions without conscious intention.' Whenever you need to locate a missing queen, you do so with speed, no apparent thought and almost inevitable success."

"Then you'll be amazed to learn that I have programmed Andy to play even better than I do."

Nomash stared incredulously at the famous bridge player. Andy was Dallow's personal android, a class A majordomo.

Dallow touched a control on his bracelet. "Would you like a demonstration?"

"Very much."

The android entered and bowed elegantly to Dallow and his guest. But for a tiny identification scar on the left earlobe, it could have been mistaken for a human manservant. Nomash was secretly jealous of its distinguished appearance.

Dallow said, "How about a little bridge, Andy?"

"I would like that very much, Par." The resonant voice was courteous, but Nomash was surprised at the use of its master's first name.

Dallow turned to his guest. "I'm sure you have one or two problems up your sleeve."

"As a matter of fact, I have. Have you a pack of cards?"

"He doesn't need them, Jord. Just tell us the hands."

"Sure. As declarer, you hold:"

♠ AQ4
♡ AKQJ
◇ QJ10987
♣ —

Andy's response was instantaneous: "I win West's ♣K lead with dummy's ♣A."

Nomash gasped in disbelief. "But how on earth ... ?"

"Tell us both hands, Jord," Dallow laughed. "Then Andy will explain."

Nomash mechanically recited the North hand:

♠ –
♡ 109876
◊ AK
♣ A98764

♠ AQ4
♡ AKQJ
◊ QJ10987
♣ –

"South to make 7♡ against any distribution. East plays the ♣2 on West's ♣K lead."

Andy said, "The key play is to discard a diamond on dummy's ♣A. I use two heart entries to ruff my low spades and play two more hearts, throwing a diamond from the table. I discard the second diamond on my ♠A, and my hand is high."

"And you worked that out in one micro-second?"

"Not at all. This is a sure tricks problem, devised two centuries ago by Harry A. Boardman. Had it not been present in my extensive databank, I would have needed almost three micro-seconds."

Dallow said, "Why not try him with a 'flair' problem, Jord? Perhaps locating a queen."

"Very well." Nomash called out the hands of declarer and dummy.

♠ AJ985
♡ 94
◊ 743
♣ 875

♠ K2
♡ A63
◊ AK85
♣ AK32

West	North	East	South
–	–	–	2NT
Pass	3♣(i)	Pass	3NT(ii)
All Pass			

(i) 5 card Stayman
(ii) 2-3 or 2-2 in the majors

"West leads the ♡5. East contributes the ♡K."

Andy said, "I hold up twice."

Nomash grinned. "I see you've played before. East continues with the ♡J and ♡7, West following with the ♡2 and ♡8. You are in with the ♡A."

"I play the ♠K."

"On which East drops the ♠10. And why aren't you calling me sir?"

"I am programmed to do so as a butler. As a bridge player, I am allowed to address humans as equals, or as the case may be, inferiors."

Nomash chose to ignore what may have been a veiled insult. "Anyway, do you finesse the ♠J, or play for the queen to drop?"

Andy asked, "Who is East?"

"Let's say another android."

"Class?"

"C."

"I would not sit down against such inferior opposition."

"But suppose you did?"

"Then I would obviously play for the drop. I cannot make the four spade tricks I need if the ♠10 is singleton. So I must assume the class C machine is following its elementary programme by playing low from the ♠Q10. In other words, that it is like most human players."

"You really are insufferably arrogant."

"Thank you. Par has given me all the qualities of a leading expert."

"And how would you play if East was also an expert?"

"That would depend on his style. If he were an incorrigibly spectacular player, I would take the marked finesse."

"Marked?"

"Of course. Dealt ♠Q10, a 'flair' player would drop the queen, hoping to induce me to finesse the nine on the next round. Holding ♠ 10xx, he would drop the ten, hoping to induce me to play for the drop. Most humans are very predictable."

Nomash glanced at Dallow, who was clearly enjoying his android's performance.

Nomash said, "But what if East were the unpredictable Par Dallow? Now you have to guess, do you not?"

"Not at all. Who is West in this rather trivial scenario?"

"Suppose he is our proverbial C class android."

"Then he will automatically give a count. If he follows upwards we finesse, if he plays high-low, we play for the drop."

"But what would you do if both defenders were great players."

The android produced a perfectly executed sneer. "At last, a moderately interesting question. In theory, one should finesse, regardless of which card East plays on the ♠ K."

"Why?"

"Forgive me. I had assumed you were class A. The theory provides that if East plays the queen it is a restricted choice position, meaning that a top class player holding the ♠ Q10 might play either card, but with the ♠ 10xx he will definitely play the ten."

"So it's a purely mathematical decision."

"Not in practice. A genuine master will usually try to deceive declarer. Holding Qxx, he will peter. With four small, he will follow upwards."

"But surely," Nomash protested, a truly expert player will vary his plays."

"Not so. My memory banks show that on two hundred and five occasions when this combination occurred in important bridge, only eleven West's signalled truly from four small cards."

"Incredible.

"I suggest that vanity lies behind the desire to play the 'correct' deceptive card and overcomes the players better judgement."

Dallow said, "Andy's right, Jord. Imagine reading in a tournament report: 'Jord Nomash petered naïvely to present declarer with his contract.

"But you are different, Par. You vary your play randomly."

"Perhaps. But it makes no difference to a class A, does it, Andy?"

"No, Par. A human giving false information might fool another human, but not an encephalograph. And I can sense not only the action of the brain but the pulse rates, eye movement, surface temperature .... Shall I go on?"

Nomash threw up his hands in dismay. "No! Pulse rates are bad enough."

"Yours is eighty-six, thirteen above your norm."

"Monstrous!"

"It is now ninety -five."

"And totally unethical."

"Why? It is only what you term 'table presence'. Humans sense an opponent's tension subconsciously. This accounts for most of what you call 'flair', and its possessors are just those who are extrasensitive to non-verbal communication."

Nomash sighed. "I suppose you must have a very poor opinion of humans."

"Not at all. After all, you designed *me*."

"May God forgive us! And that is enough bridge for this evening." He shook his head sadly.

The android's expression arranged itself in a superb combination of compassion and subservience: "May I fetch you another drink, sir?"

28
GAMESMANSHIP

Stephen Potter gave to the English language the words 'gamesmanship', 'brinkmanship', 'lifemanship' and 'one-upmanship'. Gamesmanship was the first book in the Lifemanship series, and it struck a chord with everyone who had lost a game to an opponent of markedly inferior skill and never quite knew why?

He also coined the expression 'split bridgemanship', to describe a series of plays and gambits to sow dissension among one's opponents, and devised by advanced students of the Yeovil School of Lifemanship.

Bridgemanship

Bridgemanship, like all branches of gamesmanship, is the Art of Winning Without Actually Cheating. The skilled bridgeman makes his opponents feel either one down, or dangerously one-up, and thus prone to those careless lapses which result from over-confidence.

It is in the latter field that two of our advanced graduates, J. Fortescue and Ivy Hart, have broken new ground. The EBU has rendered a grave disservice to bridgemanship by publishing lists of master point holders and tournament results, and this has partially neutralised the old one-up strategies, which can have disastrous results:

Bridgeman:	I played a similar hand against Tony and Raymond the other day.
Layman:	Oh? Was that in the Gold Cup or Crockfords?
Bridgeman:	Neither actually. It was …
Layman:	Ah! Then you must mean Tony Blenkinsop and Ray Pratt. They came fifth in our tennis club pairs.

Hart/Fortescue have struck back in true Yeovil fashion. They now cultivate an image of bumbling incompetence, implying a level of opposition scarely worth bothering about. This is particularly effective in away matches.

They invariably arrive late, apologising profusely for losing their way. When their hostess points out she faxed them a map, they produce a totally illegible facsimile, which was actually produced on a broken down photocopier, circa 1950.

The other pair arrive even later and equally apologetic. They are the twins, Bernard and Ruth, skinny impecunious teenagers, who carry copies of *Bridge for Total Beginners* with a dozen paper bookmarks, all protruding *from the first two chapters.* They look cold and hungry and on several occasions have been offered hot soup.

After the teams have been introduced, J. Fortescue employs his first gambit.

J. Fortescue: I wondered if we could use one of your rooms for a short team meeting. I'll have to work out some sort of system.

Home Captain: Oh! Haven't you played together before?

J. Fortescue: Yes, but Ivy and I thought this evening we'd, er split up the youngsters.

Home Captain: Right, we'll pop next door then.

Ivy: *(Loudly, while the captain is within earshot)* Now, kids, the first thing to remember is that it's four points for an ace, three for a king ...

This lays the foundation for Ruth's Bimbo Gambit, used when an opponent has made an overtrick by a simple throw-in.

Ruth: Gosh! Was that a squeeze?

Declarer: No, it was an endplay, actually.

Ruth: You must be awfully advanced. Bernard and I are just learning finesses. I don't suppose you bother with them.

Declarer: Well, I ...

Ruth: Ivy says you can always tell an expert by the way he avoids finessing.

For the rest of the match, the declarer rejects every finesse, flooring cold contracts by attempting precarious brilliancies. His partner's mounting disapproval provides an opening for J. Fortescue's, Let You and Him Fight Ploy.

Dummy:	That was sheer butchery.
Declarer:	I didn't play it to the best advantage.
Dummy:	You played like an ox.
J. Fortescue:	*(Placatingly)* Oh, I don't know ...
Dummy:	What?
J. Fortescue:	Only that it did look as though the finesse might be wrong, particularly when I dropped the nine. I might have gone for the squeeze myself.
Dummy:	But you opened one no trump. You had to have the bloody queen!
J. Fortescue:	Declarer may have been influenced by my shaded bids on boards three and five.
Declarer:	*(To partner)*Exactly. The trouble with you, Vicar ...

Half time often provides scope for Ivy's Food Parcel gambit, which can be devastating when the home team have offered nothing better than tea and an Osborne biscuit.

Ivy:	Tea! How kind of you. We thought you might give us tea, so we've brought you some bits and pieces.

(She produces two boxes of Harrod's mixed cream cakes)

Hostess:	*(Embarrassed)* Really. there was no need ...
Ivy:	Nonsense, least we could do. I know how expensive good tea is. Tesco's Own Brand, isn't it?

The stratagem is not as costly as it seems, as the hosts are usually too ashamed to eat anything and the Fortescue team enter the second half gastronomically, as well as morally, one-up.

By now, Ruth has adopted the expert declarer as her uncle. He has not noticed that her defensive misplays are confined to cold contracts.

Ruth:	I mucked that up, Uncle Ron.
Declarer:	I thought you defended quite well.
Ruth:	Did I really?
Declarer:	Yes, except – not that it mattered – but you might have led from the top of your sequence.
Ruth:	Is the J108 a sequence?

Declarer:	Yes, dear. So is QJ9 and KQ10 and -
Vicar:	For God's sake, Ron! We're fifty IMPs down!

Bernard reported some interesting results from his Overbid Inducement Ploy, usually launched when dummy goes down.

Bernard:	What a great bid! Shut us out completely.
Dummy:	*(Flattered)* Well, at favourable vulnerability ...
Bernard:	I wonder whether I'll ever have the nerve to bid like that?
Ivy:	You stick to what we've taught you, Bernard. Leave advanced stuff like that to the experts.

As a result of Ivy's advanced 'mother play', the victim, in order to maintain his reputation as a buccaneering grand master, has been known to bid unmakeable games on three out of the next five boards.

It cannot be sufficiently stressed that none of these bids should be doubled. Plus fifty is better than minus one-forty, and to double is not only unsporting, but will expose the nature of the ploy.

As I write, good work is being done by several of our members.

Bridgemanship is an ever-developing Art. As experts contrive more sophisticated bids and plays, bridgemen and women rise heroically to each new challenge. Multi-coloured ploys are needed to counter multi-coloured bids. And whatever the future may hold, we at Yeovil will be ready.

29
PALOOKAS ALL

The Classic Aces All *contained seventeen essays on famous stars by Guy Ramsey. In his foreword, he estimated that there were 3,000,000 bridge players in Britain. These included 1,000 good players, 500 experts and perhaps 50 masters.*

These figures reveal the deficiency of an otherwise excellent book, that it ignores the talents of 2,998,450 players who could not be described as good. These are the real heroes and heroines of the bridge world, for just as we cannot conceive of joy without the knowledge of suffering, so there can be no experts without palookas to provide comparison.

It is true that some authors write enthusiastically about bad players, but Mrs Guggenheim, the Rueful Rabbit, Brother Aelred and Godzilla are usually depicted as objects of ridicule. It is high time that the average or below-average club player is recognised as a worthy subject for learned analysis.

The Dynamic Duo: George and Edna Gummidge

George Gummidge has a loud, cheerful voice, a wide range of hand-knitted cardigans and, the reward for twenty years of success in EBU Congresses, thirteen green points. His wife, Edna, has a worried expression, which intensifies whenever she sits down to partner George, a ubiquitous bag of knitting and fourteen green points.

Members of their bridge club have been trying for years to discover the source of that extra point. Has she been unfaithful to George? Unthinkable. They are as inseparable as ham and eggs, or Koch and Werner.

George is widely regarded as the clearest thinker in the fourth division of the local league. He plays with two clearly defined objectives: to play ninety percent of the contracts and to win one hundred per cent of the post mortems.

His dedicated pursuit of the first of these goals has led to the development of the celebrated (though unlicensed) Gummidge Systems. That George and Edna require more than one is demonstrated in situations such as the following:

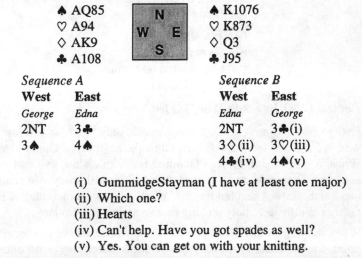

	♠ AQ5		♠ K86
	♡ K1094		♡ QJ7
	◇ Q65		◇ A982
	♣ K108		♣ Q95

Sequence A		*Sequence B*	
West	**East**	**West**	**East**
George	*Edna*	*Edna*	*George*
1NT	3NT	1♣	2NT
		3NT	

Edna opens one no trump only when she has no suit longer than three. On the only occasion when she did venture such an opening, it was belatedly discovered that she had been dealt twelve cards. When she held such hands as ♠AJ94 ♡AJ96 ◇K8 ♣1095, the partnership found the difficulty in rightsiding the contract almost insuperable, until George had the inspiration of incorporating the Precision Diamond into Edna's version of Acol.

Two no trump openings posed a further challenge to George's ingenuity, but he responded by inventing Gummidge Stayman:

	♠ AQ85		♠ K1076
	♡ A94		♡ K873
	◇ AK9		◇ Q3
	♣ A108		♣ J95

Sequence A		*Sequence B*	
West	**East**	**West**	**East**
George	*Edna*	*Edna*	*George*
2NT	3♣	2NT	3♣(i)
3♠	4♠	3◇(ii)	3♡(iii)
		4♣(iv)	4♠(v)

(i)   GummidgeStayman (I have at least one major)
(ii) Which one?
(iii) Hearts
(iv) Can't help. Have you got spades as well?
(v)   Yes. You can get on with your knitting.

Even Gummidge Stayman has its drawbacks, but George maintains that the rare occasions when he has to play at the four level in a four-two fit are a small price to pay for a huge advance in scientific bidding.

Edna opens five card majors, George opens with four. To compensate, she raises with three card support, while he raises with five. It is hardly surprising that, as a result of such elegant bidding, George has become the most practised declarer in the district. Here is an example of his technique:

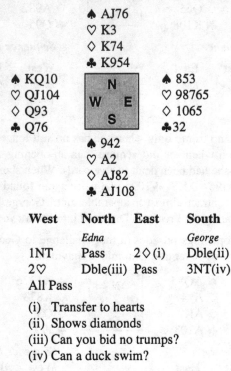

```
                    ♠ AJ76
                    ♡ K3
                    ◇ K74
                    ♣ K954
      ♠ KQ10                      ♠ 853
      ♡ QJ104        N            ♡ 98765
      ◇ Q93       W     E         ◇ 1065
      ♣ Q76          S            ♣ 32
                    ♠ 942
                    ♡ A2
                    ◇ AJ82
                    ♣ AJ108
```

West	North	East	South
	Edna		*George*
1NT	Pass	2◇(i)	Dble(ii)
2♡	Dble(iii)	Pass	3NT(iv)
All Pass			

(i)   Transfer to hearts
(ii) Shows diamonds
(iii) Can you bid no trumps?
(iv) Can a duck swim?

Contract 3NT by South. The ♡ Q led.

George scorned any notion of an esoteric play, such as a throw-in. He won in hand and led the ♣J. Now came the key play, a Gummidge Coup. When West covered, George favoured her with a slow shake of the head and a pitying smile as he played the ♣K from dummy. He returned to hand with the ♣A and led the ◇J. West, a quick learner, played low and George ran the jack; duly making twelve tricks for a cold top.

When, hoping to discover the clue to the source of her fourteenth green point, I asked Edna for an example of her declarer play in no trumps, she was unable to recall one. Instead, she gave me details of all five of her suit contracts, in which her speciality is the cross-ruff. Here is a grand slam, which she made with thirteen ruffs, sitting West in the annual flitch.

Edna
♠ AKQJ1098
♡ AKQJ109
◇ –
♣ –

George
♠ 765432
♡ –
◇ AKQJ1043
♣ –

The bidding was unremarkable, as George's final bid of 8◇ was disallowed. Edna was justly proud of achieving an average score, and although George was initially critical of certain aspects of the auction, he relented on discovering that diamonds broke six-nil.

I asked them both for some examples of their defence, but they modestly declined. George suggested that I should save it for a follow-up article, possibly when they became Regional Masters. I am sure that their many friends are united in hoping that day is not too far off.

30
WATERSHIP DOWN

It has been said that nobody who reads this remarkable novel by Richard Adams will ever again feel the same about rabbits.

This of course raises the question: How do rabbits feel about us? How, for example, would they feel about reviewing the last pastiche in this book, which features Victor Mollo's Rueful Rabbit.

The Rabbit's Birthday Treat.

The Rueful Rabbit munched contentedly at a chocolate almond biscuit. He was the Hideous Hog's partner against two nondescript players from the Midlands. He had contributed to three successful defences by accidentally playing several correct cards, and watched HH make a routine small slam with a criss-cross squeeze and four finesses. He was brimming with confidence as he dealt with the following hand:

Game All. Dealer South.

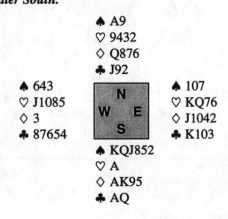

```
                    ♠ A9
                    ♡ 9432
                    ◊ Q876
                    ♣ J92
    ♠ 643                        ♠ 107
    ♡ J1085         N            ♡ KQ76
    ◊ 3          W     E         ◊ J1042
    ♣ 87654         S            ♣ K103
                    ♠ KQJ852
                    ♡ A
                    ◊ AK95
                    ♣ AQ
```

West	North	East	South
	The Hog		*The Rabbit*
-	-	-	2◇
Pass	2NT	Pass	3♠
Pass	4◇	Pass	4NT
Pass	5◇	Pass	7◇
Pass	Pass	Dble	Rdbl
All Pass			

The auction was a fine example of RR's versatility. Having been playing Benjamin two bids with the Toucan, he absent-mindedly opened 2◇ to show 23 or more points. The Hog took this to be an Acol two, showing eight playing tricks. RR's redouble was a show of confidence in the Hog, whom he thought would be playing the contract.

When the ♡J appeared from West, a crimson flush spread slowly upwards from the Rabbit's neck. Winning with the ♡A, he squared his round shoulders and manfully addressed the task of going down as few as possible.

Oscar the Owl, the Senior Kibitzer, could see that declarer needed a successful club finesse, and – if East held the ◇J10xx –. two finesses in trumps. The problem was that he only had two entries to the table.

The RR's analysis was more advanced. Should he reel off the spades and squeeze everybody till their pips rattled? Or contrive a miraculous end-play?

"Stop thinking, RR," the Hog chortled. "Just play the card with the denomination nearest your birthday. It's probably as good as anything."

"It would serve you right if I did!" cried the Rabbit. He defiantly selected the ◇9 and took with dummy's queen. Oscar gasped at the ingenuity of the Rabbit's unblocking play. RR now led the ◇8, and covered East's ◇10 with the king. He re-entered dummy with the ♠A and led the ◇7. East did his best by rising with the ◇J, won by declarer's ace. The Owl held his breath as the Rabbit considered his next play, and then, achieving an unprecedented feat of memory, crossed to the master ◇6 and triumphantly took the winning club finesse.

Later, at the bar, I invited the Hog to comment – in the strictest confidence – on the remarkable advice he had given the Rabbit.

"It was obvious," HH replied, "that the contract was in danger if East held the ◇J10xx, in which case declarer needed to hold the ◇9, and of course to unblock it. As I held the other three nines, even he could hardly go wrong."

"Well," I said acidly, "I can only hope that Oscar doesn't report you for your flagrant breach of ethics."

"Breach of ethics?" exclaimed the Hog. "I was merely trying to compensate for my unforgivable error. I should of course bid 7NT, and played the contract myself. So having put the Rabbit in such a predicament, it was my humanitarian duty to extricate him."

"Very well," I said grudgingly, "But what puzzles me, HH, is that you of all people could possibly know that RR was born on the ninth."

"You dare to imply that I am not profoundly interested in my fellow men!" he barked. "It so happened that he gave us a superb dinner to celebrate his last birthday, and I had chivalrously made a diary note to remind him that his next was imminent."

His arrogance evaporated as he swallowed the remainder of my antique brandy. "And after that rubber of 42," he said, "I think I can afford to give us a Mouton Rothschild."

"Well," Fiver asked. "What do you think of it?"

"I don't understand it," said Hazell. "Is this Rueful Rabbit supposed to be the hero, or isn't he?"

"Humans aren't like us. Their stories don't always have heroes."

"Rubbish!" snorted Bigwig. "How can you have a story without a hero?"

"Well he does come out on top," said Fiver. "In that respect he's a bit like us. And I suppose we're heroes."

"But we always know what we're doing," Hazell objected. "He only managed with the help of the Hog. Perhaps he's the hero."

"Impossible," said Bigwig. "A hog can't be the hero of a rabbit story. It doesn't make sense."

"Have you noticed?" Fiver mused. "RR is always bringing off these trump squeezes and things. Do you think he really does it all deliberately?"

Bigwig stared at him. "That's ridiculous. How can a rabbit know about bridge coups? People have enough trouble with the idea of you and Hazell sailing boats and taming seagulls."

"You're right, Bigwig," Hazell agreed. "Let's go up and silflay.

"What's all this silflay nonsense? Why can't you say 'eat' like everybody else?"